DK

T0201830

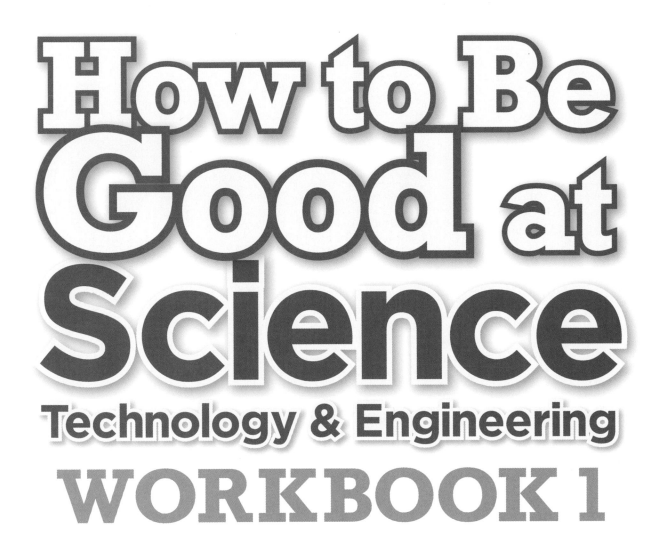

How to Be Good at Science
Technology & Engineering
WORKBOOK 1

The **simplest-ever** visual workbook

DK | Penguin Random House

Produced for DK by
Dynamo Limited
1 Cathedral Court, Southernhay East, Exeter, EX1 1AF

Authors Susan House
Consultant Courtney Mayer

Senior Editor Ankita Awasthi Tröger
Senior Art Editor Amy Child
Editors Lizzie Munsey, Catharine Robertson
US Editor Heather Wilcox
Designer Anna Scully
Managing Editor Christine Stroyan
Managing Art Editor Anna Hall
Senior Production Editor Andy Hilliard
Senior Production Controller Samantha Cross
Jacket Design Development Manager Sophia MTT
Jacket Designer Tanya Mehrotra
DTP Designer Rakesh Kumar
Publisher Andrew Macintyre
Associate Publishing Director Liz Wheeler
Art Director Karen Self
Publishing Director Jonathan Metcalf

First American Edition, 2021
Published in the United States by DK Publishing
1450 Broadway, Suite 801, New York, NY 10018

Copyright © 2021 Dorling Kindersley Limited
DK, a Division of Penguin Random House LLC
21 22 23 24 25   10 9 8 7 6 5 4 3 2 1
001–322112–Oct/2021

All rights reserved.
Without limiting the rights under the copyright reserved above, no part of this
publication may be reproduced, stored in or introduced into a retrieval system, or
transmitted, in any form, or by any means (electronic, mechanical, photocopying,
recording, or otherwise), without the prior written permission of the copyright owner.
Published in Great Britain by Dorling Kindersley Limited

A catalog record for this book
is available from the Library of Congress.
ISBN 978-0-7440-2887-4

DK books are available at special discounts when purchased
in bulk for sales promotions, premiums, fund-raising, or educational use.
For details, contact: DK Publishing Special Markets, 1450 Broadway,
Suite 801, New York, NY 10018
SpecialSales@dk.com

Printed and bound in China

All images © Dorling Kindersley. For further information, visit **www.dkimages.com**.

For the curious
www.dk.com

This book was made with Forest Stewardship Council ™ certified
paper—one small step in DK's commitment to a sustainable future.

For more information go to www.dk.com/our-green-pledge

Contents

Forces

Earth and space

📖 Pages 000–000

The page numbers next to this icon refer to pages in DK's *How to Be Good at Science*.

How science works

In science, we discover facts about the world. We test our ideas and discover new facts by doing experiments.

REMEMBER!
For experiments, scientists follow six steps called the scientific method.

1 Use the words in the word box to help you fill in the six steps of the scientific method.

analyze results	make an observation	do an experiment
form a hypothesis	collect data	repeat the experiment

a   Step 1: _____ _____

Why is the grass taller in some places than in others?

b   Step 2: _____ _____

Maybe the cow manure makes the grass grow better.

c   Step 3: _____ _____

We need to test our theory.

100% soil
80% soil
20% manure
50% soil
50% manure

d   Step 4: _____ _____

This plant is really healthy. It's grown more than the others.

80% soil
20% manure

e   Step 5: _____ _____

Look carefully at the results from the experiment.

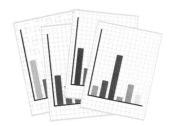

f   Step 6: _____ _____

Do the experiment again to check that the results are right.

2 Scientists test their ideas by following a sequence of steps that form the scientific method. Number these sentences to show the correct order of the steps.

a   Use measuring instruments. ☐

b   Have a hunch or idea. ☐

c   Make an observation. ☐

d   Test out their hunches. ☐

e   Draw graphs. ☐

f   Check again. ☐

3 Draw lines to match each term with the correct meaning.

a (Observation)   (an explanation for something)

b (Hypothesis)   (look and notice something)

c (Experiment)   (examine something carefully)

d (Data)   (do something again)

e (Analyze)   (test to find something out)

f (Repeat)   (facts and figures)

4 Conduct an experiment to test whether plants need sunlight to grow. Then answer the questions below, using the picture to help you.

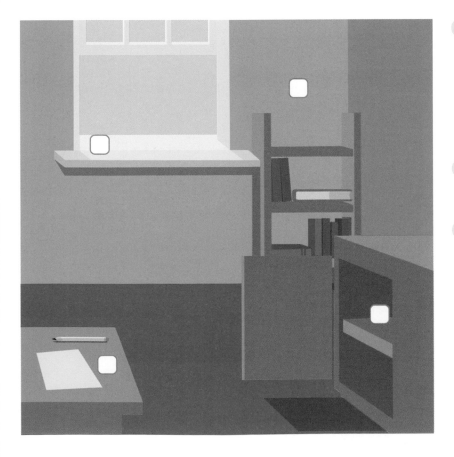

a What equipment would you need for an experiment to test whether plants need sunlight to grow?

_____

_____

b Where would the plant get the most light? Check two boxes.

c Choose where you think your plant would grow best. Write a sentence to explain why.

_____

_____

_____

_____

_____

📖 Pages 10–11

Working scientifically

Working scientifically means asking questions, carrying out tests, and collecting data. When we do scientific experiments, we often use special equipment to help us measure things accurately.

We use thermometers to measure temperature.

We use scales to weigh solids.

We use cylinders to measure liquids.

1 Use the key to help you say which piece of equipment would be used to measure each of the objects below.

Key   C Cylinder   S Scales

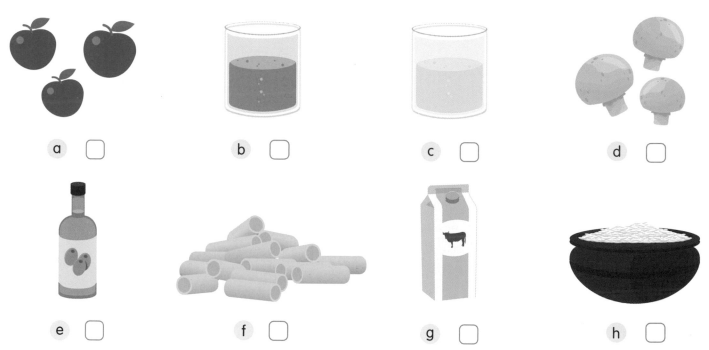

a ☐   b ☐   c ☐   d ☐

e ☐   f ☐   g ☐   h ☐

2 When scientists measure something, they try to be both accurate and precise. Read the statements below and check the one that is both accurate and precise.

a   You weigh some sugar twice with the same scales, getting the same result. With new scales, you get a different result.   ☐

b   You weigh some sugar four times, and each time you get a slightly different result.   ☐

c   You weigh some sugar four times on two different sets of scales, and you always get the same result.   ☐

REMEMBER!
When we are measuring, the word "precise" means you get the same result or measurement each time. The word "accurate" means the result matches the real value.

3 Read these statements about how scientists work and then circle true (T) or false (F) for each.

a Scientists always work alone.   T / F

b Scientific theories never get overturned.   T / F

c Scientists compete with each other to be the first to prove theories.   T / F

d Scientists share their findings by publishing them.   T / F

e Scientists have to be very methodical so they don't make mistakes.   T / F

f Scientists use the work of other experts to build their theories.   T / F

4 Think about how you can make sure that your measurements are accurate and precise. Check the suggestions below that you agree with.

a Check your equipment against other equipment.

b Compare your measurements with a friend.

c Repeat your measurements several times.

d Ask your friend to do the measuring for you.

e If you are using scales, check that they return to zero after weighing.

SCIENCE AT HOME

Ready, set, go!

"Bias" in science experiments is when errors creep into measurements. Try this experiment to test bias.

1. Ask two people at home to help you. You will each need a timer (you can use the one on a cell phone).

2. Set all three timers to 30 seconds. Ask one person to call out "start." As soon as they call out, everyone should start their own timer. Repeat this step, taking turns being the caller.

3. Then complete this table. What bias do you notice?

Who called out "start"?	Whose timer finished first?

Fields of science

Biology, chemistry, and physics are the three main fields of science. Some scientists also study space and Earth.

REMEMBER!
Scientific instruments are the tools scientists use for their work.

1 Circle nine words about the study of biology in the word search below. Use the words in the word box to help you.

zoology

botany

ecology

cells

environment

microbiology

medicine

disease

organism

t	f	e	z	o	o	l	o	g	y	t	y	u	a
r	m	i	c	r	o	b	i	o	l	o	g	y	d
a	e	a	d	g	f	g	b	h	j	c	k	e	n
o	d	z	x	a	c	v	o	b	n	e	m	c	e
p	i	u	y	n	t	r	t	e	w	l	q	o	r
r	c	i	d	i	s	e	a	s	e	l	o	l	f
a	i	f	g	s	h	j	n	k	l	s	p	o	c
h	n	d	s	m	a	z	y	x	c	v	b	g	a
y	e	n	v	i	r	o	n	m	e	n	t	y	u

Then, use some of the same words to help you complete these sentences.

a _____ is the study of animals, and _____ is the study of plants.

b _____ is the study of the environment, which shows us how living things interact.

c In _____ , we use a microscope to study _____ , which make up all living things.

d In _____ , we study different diseases that affect humans to keep people healthy.

e An _____ is a living thing, such as a plant or an animal.

f The _____ is all the living and nonliving things that surround us.

2 Use the words in the word box to help you answer the questions below.

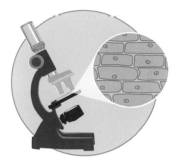

| biology |
| chemistry |
| Earth science |
| physics |
| space science |

a   Which field studies cells?

_____

b   Which field studies forces and energy?

_____

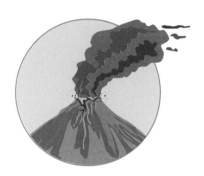
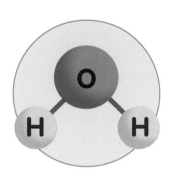

c   Which field studies planets and stars?

_____

d   Which field studies volcanoes and earthquakes?

_____

e   Which field studies atoms and molecules?

_____

3 Draw lines to match each field of science with the sentence that describes it.

a	b	c	d	e
Biology	Chemistry	Earth science	Physics	Space science

| invents a new nonstick pan. | calculates the force needed to move an object. | studies the relationship between plants and animals in an environment. | finds new planets and galaxies. | identifies the rocks in a specific place. |

📖 Pages 14–15

How engineering works

Engineers solve specific human problems by inventing or constructing something. There are four main types of engineer: chemical, civil, mechanical, and electrical.

1 Use the words in the word box to help you identify the engineer who does the type of work described below.

a   Design a new tunnel for the railroad: _____ engineer

b   Calculate data for a new computer chip: _____ engineer

c   Design a robot for a car factory: _____ engineer

d   Make products from oil: _____ engineer

> chemical
>
> civil
>
> electrical
>
> mechanical

2 Use the words from the word box in question 1 to help you identify the type of engineer who invented each object labeled in this picture.

a   Building: _____

b   Computers: _____

c   Elevator: _____

d   Gas pumps: _____

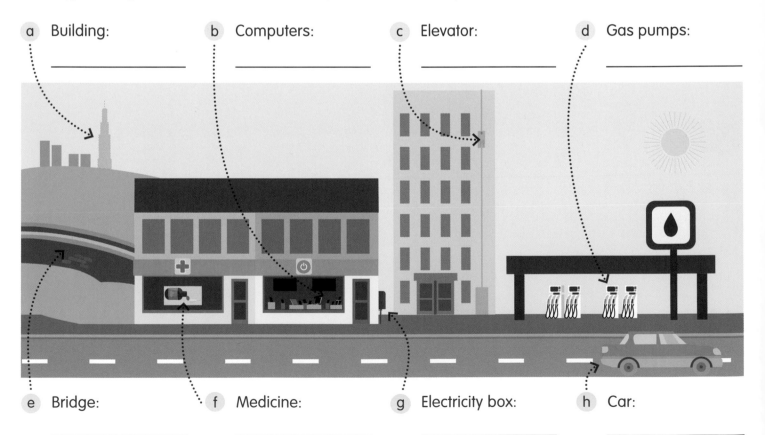

e   Bridge: _____

f   Medicine: _____

g   Electricity box: _____

h   Car: _____

3 In this word snake, circle six words about the stages of the engineering design process. Use the words in the word box to help you.

| test   model   ask   share   imagine   plan |

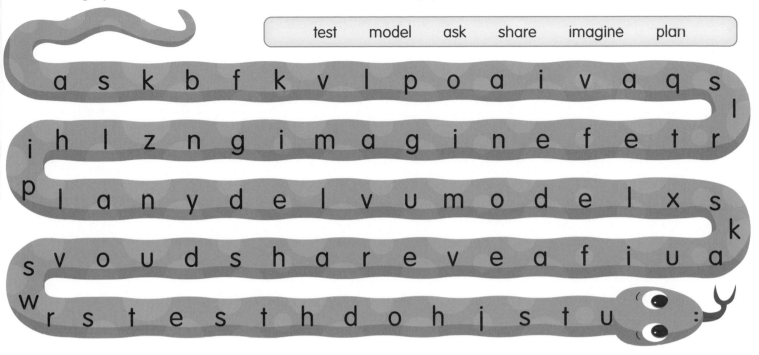

4 Use the words from the word box in question 3 to help you complete these sentences about the engineering design process.

a Identify a problem and _____ questions about it.

b _____ different solutions to the problem.

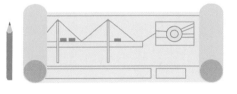

c _____ the best solutions and draw diagrams.

d Build a _____ .

e _____ the model and improve on your design.

f _____ your ideas.

Pages 16–17

What is life?

There are millions of living things in the world. Some are very small, like germs, and others are huge, like big trees. Animals and plants look very different, but they share certain characteristics.

REMEMBER!
Living things are also called organisms.

1 Use the words "all" or "some" to complete these sentences.

a _____ organisms share some characteristics.

b _____ organisms urinate to remove waste.

c _____ organisms eat other organisms.

d _____ organisms lay eggs to reproduce.

e _____ organisms need energy.

f _____ organisms grow over time.

g _____ organisms move by using muscles.

h _____ can sense things in their surroundings.

2 These pictures show seven things living organisms need to do in order to survive. Use the words in the word box to help you label the pictures.

get energy

reproduce   grow

get food   move

sense surroundings

remove waste

a _____

b _____

c _____

d _____

e _____

f _____

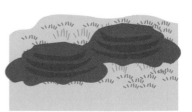

g _____

3 Classify each of these phrases by writing "H" if it refers to the horses, "T" if it refers to the trees, or "B" if it refers to both.

a   Move by using muscles ☐

b   Use energy ☐

c   Urinate ☐

d   Roots grow down ☐

e   Give birth ☐

f   Get bigger ☐

g   Sense things in their surroundings ☐

h   Create seeds ☐

> **REMEMBER!**
> Although plants and animals look very different, all organisms share certain characteristics.

Living things

Complete this table with living things found in your home. Then, answer the questions below.

Animals	Plants
Me	

Do all the living things in your home grow in exactly the same way?

_____

_____

Which living things in your home feed on other organisms?

_____

_____

Which living things in your home can run?

_____

_____

📖 Pages 20–21

Classification

Living organisms are classified into groups according to their common characteristics.

1 Draw lines to match each organism with the correct characteristics.

a   Animals

c   Fungi

absorb food from organic matter.

have sense organs, are multicellular, and eat other organisms.

are microscopic, and some are single-celled.

are multicellular, produce their own food, and have roots.

b   Plants

d   Microorganisms

2 Use some of the words from the characteristics in question 1 to complete these definitions. You will need to use some words more than once.

a _____ means to soak up or take in some type of liquid.

b _____ means that an organism has more than one cell.

c _____ means that an organism has only one cell.

d _____ means that you can only see it with a microscope.

e _____ comes from the remains of animals, plants, and their waste products.

3 Read these sentences about invertebrates and then circle true (T) or false (F) for each.

a Invertebrates are animals that don't have a backbone.   T / F

b Most of the animal species in the world are vertebrates.   T / F

c Some invertebrates have shells.   T / F

d Invertebrates are all land animals.   T / F

e Some invertebrates can fly.   T / F

f All invertebrates have legs.   T / F

4 Tick the correct columns in this table to complete the information about vertebrates.

	Mammals	Birds	Fish	Reptiles	Amphibians
a Warm-blooded					
b Cold-blooded					
c Dry scales					
d Wet scales					
e Slimy skin					
f Feathers					
g Fur or hair					
h Gills					
i Lay eggs in water					
j Lay eggs on land					
k Feed young with milk					

Pages 22–23

Nutrition

All living things need food. Food contains chemicals called nutrients that provide the body's cells with energy and with essential materials needed for growth and repair.

REMEMBER!
As well as needing nutrients from food, your body needs a regular supply of water.

1 These pictures show the six main types of nutrients, or food groups. Use the words in the word box to help you label them.

| carbohydrates | fiber | lipids | minerals | proteins | vitamins |

a _____

b _____

c _____

d _____

e _____

f _____

2 Different types of food do different jobs inside our bodies. Draw lines to match each food with the reason that we need it.

| are important for teeth and bones. | help repair tissues in the body. | keep our digestive system healthy. |

a Proteins   b Minerals   c Carbohydrates   d Lipids   e Fiber   f Vitamins

| provide energy for our cells. | provide small amounts of compounds we need to stay healthy. | help our body store energy. |

3 Use the words in the word box to help you describe how much these plates of food contain of each of the nutrients listed below.

| some   a lot   not a lot   none |

a Chocolate cake and ice cream

b Chicken, potatoes, and vegetables

c Curry, rice, and tomatoes

Protein: _____

Minerals: _____

Carbohydrates: _____

Vitamins: _____

Lipids: _____

Fiber: _____

Protein: _____

Minerals: _____

Carbohydrates: _____

Vitamins: _____

Lipids: _____

Fiber: _____

Protein: _____

Minerals: _____

Carbohydrates: _____

Vitamins: _____

Lipids: _____

Fiber: _____

📖 Pages 28–29

Human digestive system

Our digestive system breaks food down into small units called nutrients. These nutrients are then absorbed into our blood.

REMEMBER!
Our bodies need different types of nutrients in order to stay healthy.

1 Use the words in the word box to help you label the parts of the digestive system.

gallbladder

large intestine

liver

mouth

esophagus

pancreas

small intestine

stomach

a _____

b _____

c _____

d _____

e _____

f _____

g _____

h _____

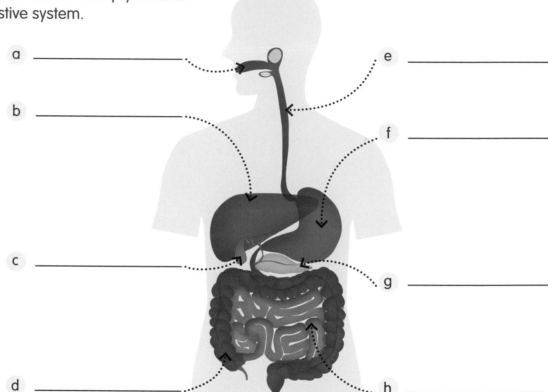

2 Circle six words about digestion in the word search below. Use the words in the word box to help you.

absorbed

enzymes   secreted

saliva   feces

peristalsis

r	o	s	s	w	t	s	i	s	x	v
c	s	e	c	r	e	t	e	d	v	q
i	r	s	a	b	s	o	r	b	e	d
y	r	y	s	a	f	e	c	e	s	w
p	e	r	i	s	t	a	l	s	i	s
n	s	a	l	i	v	a	y	u	n	s
a	d	e	n	z	y	m	e	s	p	i

3 Use the words from the word box in question 2 to help you complete these sentences. Then, number the sentences to show the correct order of the digestive process.

a Different enzymes are _____ in the small intestine. ☐

b Digestive _____ break down proteins in the stomach. ☐

c In the mouth, food is mashed and moistened with _____ . ☐

d Waste leaves the body as _____ , which is another word for poop. ☐

e Water is _____ in the large intestine. ☐

f _____ is the movement of the muscles in the esophagus. ☐

4 Draw lines to match each word with the correct explanation.

In the…   food is…

a mouth   churned up and mixed with acid.

b esophagus   mixed with enzymes that digest proteins, fats, and carbohydrates.

c stomach   pushed down a tube by muscles contracting and relaxing.

d small intestine   mashed into small pieces.

e large intestine   eliminated as waste, and water is absorbed.

5 Write a short science story to describe the journey of a sandwich through your digestive system.

a First _____

b Next _____

c Then _____

d After that _____

e Finally _____

Teeth

Our teeth are set into our jaws, which we are able to move up and down. We bite and grind food with our teeth. Different shaped teeth do different jobs.

REMEMBER!
Carnivores eat other animals, herbivores eat plants, and omnivores eat both. They have different kinds of teeth because they eat different foods.

1 Look at this diagram of types of teeth and then use the labels to complete the table below.

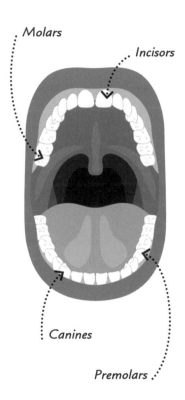

Tooth	Position	Shape	Function
a _____	front of mouth	chisel-shaped	nibbling, cutting
b _____	back of mouth	flat-topped with ridges	crunching, grinding
c _____	between incisors and premolars	pointed	biting, tearing
d _____	between molars and canines	small, flat-topped	grinding

2 Draw lines to match these sentence halves about teeth and their functions.

a (Carnivores eat)   (to kill their prey and eat the meat.)

b (Carnivores have molars)   (other animals.)

c (Carnivores need canines)   (for cutting through vegetation.)

d (Herbivores eat)   (to crunch through bones.)

e (Herbivores have molars)   (a range of plants.)

f (Herbivores need incisors)   (for grinding tough vegetation.)

3 Read these sentences about different types of teeth and then circle true (T) or false (F) for each.

a   Some herbivores don't have canines.   T / F

b   Herbivores don't need incisors.   T / F

c   Vegetation is tougher than meat.   T / F

d   Carnivores have sharp molars.   T / F

e   Omnivores have teeth that are all the same as carnivore teeth.   T / F

f   Omnivores have some teeth like carnivores and some teeth like herbivores.   T / F

4 Use the key to help you color in the types of teeth in these diagrams of dog and horse skulls.

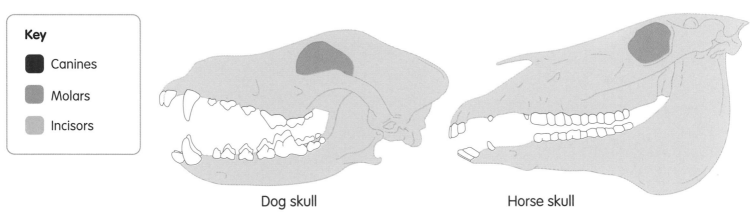

Key

■ Canines

■ Molars

■ Incisors

Dog skull   Horse skull

SCIENCE AT HOME

Tooth survey

Do a survey by asking people at home these questions.
Use their answers to complete the table.

Names			
How many teeth do you have?			
Do you have any fillings?			
When was the last time you went to the dentist?			
How often do you brush your teeth each day?			

📖 Pages 32–33

Blood

Blood is a liquid that is pumped by the heart.
It flows around the body, delivering oxygen
and nutrients and carrying away waste.

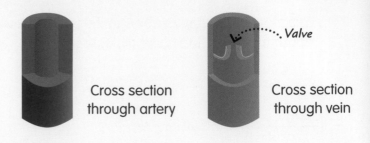

Cross section
through artery

Valve

Cross section
through vein

1 Use the key to help you color in the
arteries and veins on this diagram.

Key	⬛ Arteries	⬛ Veins

REMEMBER!
Blood flows through tubes
called arteries and veins.

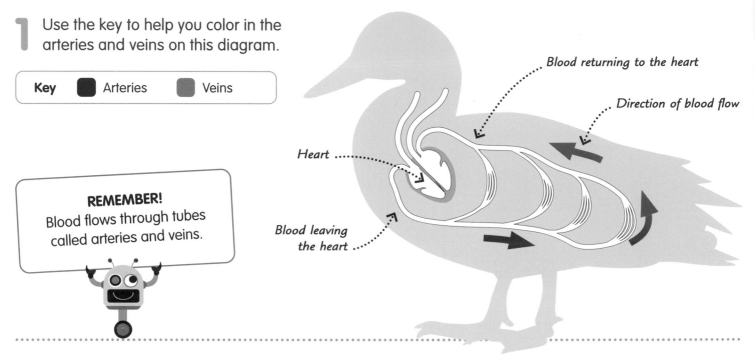

Blood returning to the heart

Direction of blood flow

Heart

Blood leaving
the heart

2 Circle seven words or phrases about the blood transportation system in the
word search below. Use the words in the word box to help you.

chambers	capillaries	heart	oxygen	veins	blood vessels	arteries

a	b	b	l	o	o	d	v	e	s	s	e	l	s	f	e	i
q	h	r	d	o	x	e	e	a	r	t	e	r	i	e	s	f
c	e	a	s	d	y	k	i	y	r	p	g	d	s	u	h	l
a	a	c	t	n	g	b	n	c	h	a	m	b	e	r	s	y
m	r	z	a	j	e	r	s	v	u	a	s	e	w	b	h	x
p	t	m	v	c	n	c	a	p	i	l	l	a	r	i	e	s

3 Use the words from the word box in question 2 to help you complete these sentences about the blood transportation system. You will need to use some words twice.

a The _____ is divided into left and right _____ .

b _____ and _____ are different types of _____ .

c _____ travel out from the _____ . _____ travel back to the _____ .

d _____ split into _____ inside the tissues.

4 Complete this table by filling in the names of the four different components of blood.

Component	a _____ _____	b _____ _____	c _____ _____	d _____ _____
Appearance	small cells	large cells	fragments of cells	yellow liquid
Function	carry oxygen around the body	protect the body from infection	help blood clot	carries nutrients and waste products around the body

5 Read these sentences about blood transfusions and check the ones that are true.

a A blood donor is a person who gives their blood to other people. ☐

b Donors don't have to be healthy. ☐

c Blood is taken from the donor, using a plastic tube inserted into a vein. ☐

d Donor blood is given to a patient who is ill or badly injured. ☐

e It doesn't matter what blood type the donor and the patient are. ☐

f The donor's blood type must match the patient's blood type. ☐

Pages 38–39

The heart

The heart is a strong muscle that pumps blood around the body. It works nonstop throughout your life.

DID YOU KNOW?
The heart beats 70 times in a minute and 40 million times in a year.

1 Circle five words about the heart in the word snake below. Use the words in the word box to help you.

| valve | vein | ventricle | atrium | artery |

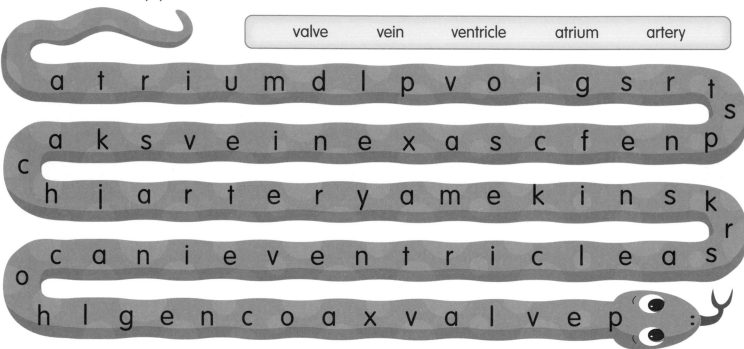

2 Use the words from the word box in question 1 to help you label this diagram of the heart. You will need to use some words twice.

a _____

b Right _____

c _____

d Right _____

e _____

f Left _____

g _____

h Left _____

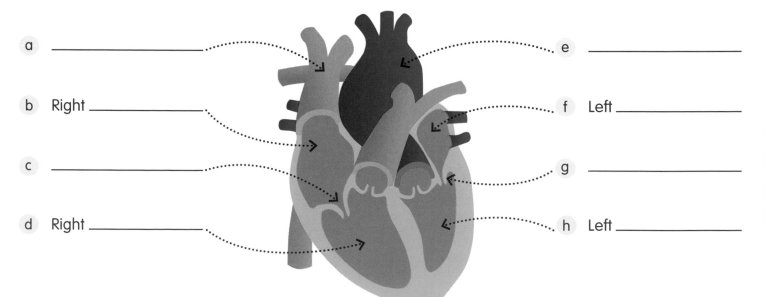

3 Draw lines to match these sentence halves about how blood is pumped around the body. Use the diagrams below to help you.

a [When the heart relaxes,]   [and blood moves out of the heart to the arteries.]

b [The atrium walls contract]   [blood from the veins fills the atria.]

c [The ventricle walls contract]   [and squeeze blood into the ventricles.]

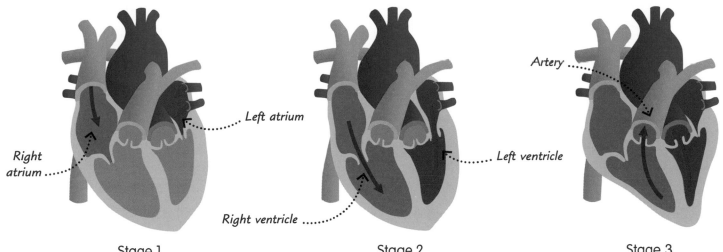

Right atrium ·····   Left atrium   Left ventricle

Right ventricle ·······   Artery ·····

Stage 1   Stage 2   Stage 3

4 Answer these questions about the heart.

a How many chambers are there in the heart, and what are they called?

_____

_____

b What happens to the blood when the heart relaxes?

_____

_____

c What happens to the blood when the heart contracts?

_____

_____

d What keeps the blood flowing in the right direction?

_____

_____

e In which direction do the veins carry blood?

_____

f In which direction do the arteries carry blood?

_____

📖 Pages 40–41

Sensing and responding

To survive, organisms must sense their surroundings and respond to food or danger. Different organisms sense and respond to the world in different ways.

REMEMBER!
Animals sense and respond faster than plants because of their nervous system and muscles.

1 Tick the correct answers to these questions about sensing and responding.

a Why do plants respond to their surroundings much more slowly than animals?

Because plants don't have muscles and a nervous system. ☐

Because plants don't detect stimuli. ☐

b Why are the sight and smell of a fox a powerful stimulus to a rabbit?

Because foxes are usual in a rabbit's environment. ☐

Because foxes are predators and a danger to rabbits. ☐

2 Use the words in the word box to help you label these pictures showing how a rabbit responds to the sight and smell of a predator.

control center	effectors	receptors
response	stimulus	

a _____

b _____

c _____

d _____

e _____

3 Circle the correct words or phrases to complete each of these sentences about how plants sense and respond to stimuli.

a   Plants **can / can't** detect light and water.

b   Plants **have / don't have** a nervous system.

c   Plants respond very **quickly / slowly** to stimuli.

d   Plants grow **toward / away from** light.

e   Tendrils are stimulated by **sound / touch.**

f   Roots **always / sometimes** grow down.

....

4 Circle the receptors that would detect the stimuli in each situation below.

a   Rotten food

| eyes | ears | nose | mouth | skin |

b   Fire

| eyes | ears | nose | mouth | skin |

c   An approaching vehicle

| eyes | ears | nose | mouth | skin |

d   Freezing ice cubes

| eyes | ears | nose | mouth | skin |

📖 Pages 46–47

The human eye

Eyes are the sense organs that allow us to see the world. They send nerve signals to the brain, where information is processed into images.

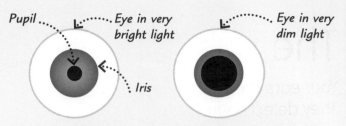

The iris controls how much light enters the eye by making the pupil smaller or bigger.

1 Use the words in the word box to help you label this diagram of the eye.

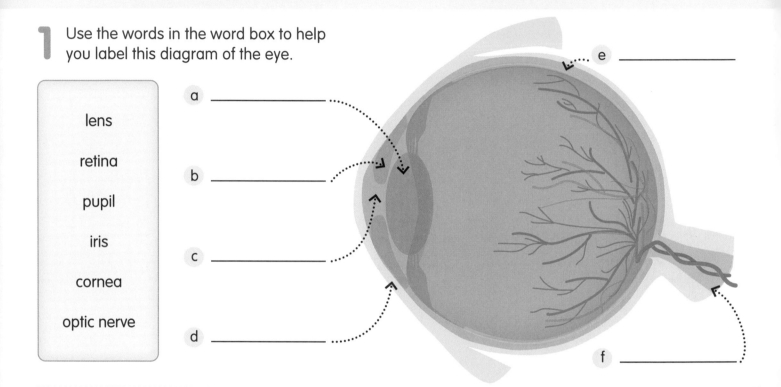

Word box:
- lens
- retina
- pupil
- iris
- cornea
- optic nerve

a _____

b _____

c _____

d _____

e _____

f _____

2 Number these sentences in the correct order to explain how our eyes perceive light.

a   The light rays are converted into nerve pulses. ☐

b   An upside-down image is formed on the retina. ☐

c   Light enters our eye through the cornea. ☐

d   The eye muscles change shape to focus the light rays. ☐

e   The nerve pulses travel along the optic nerve to the brain. ☐

f   The brain processes the nerve pulses and turns them into an image that is the right way up. ☐

g   Light-sensitive cells at the back of the retina detect the light. ☐

📖 Pages 50–51

The human ear

Your ears are your body's organs of hearing. They detect sound waves and send nerve signals to your brain, where the information is recognized as sound.

REMEMBER!
Sound is produced when an object vibrates. This causes molecules in the air to vibrate, creating a sound wave.

1 Use the words in the word box to help you label this diagram of the ear.

ossicles   cochlea   nerve   eardrum

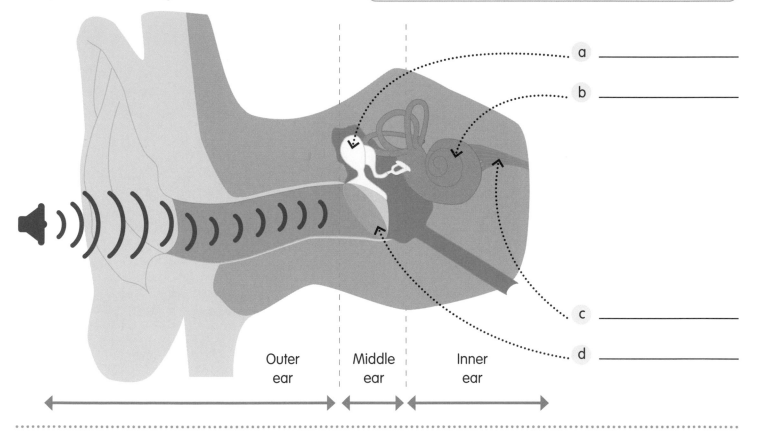

a _____

b _____

c _____

d _____

Outer ear   Middle ear   Inner ear

2 Read these descriptions of how each part of the ear helps us to hear. Then use the words from the word box in question 1 to help you identify the part of the ear described in each sentence.

a This snail-shaped tube, filled with fluid and lined with tiny hairs, detects movement:

_____

b This thin membrane vibrates when sound hits it:

_____

c This carries information about sounds to the brain:

_____

d These three tiny bones amplify sound and pass it on:

_____

How animals move

All living things can move. Animals have muscles and a nervous system that control their movements.

DID YOU KNOW?
Caterpillars have more than twice as many muscles as humans!

1 Answer these questions about animals and how they move.

a　Do all animals move?

_____

_____

b　What do muscles do to create movement?

_____

_____

c　Why can animals make bigger and faster movements than plants?

_____

_____

d　Where do animals get the energy they need for movement?

_____

_____

2 Use the words in the word box to help you complete these sentences about animals and how they move. You will need to use some words twice.

a　_____ need strong muscles in their

_____ so they can swim.

b　_____ need strong muscles in their

_____ so they can fly.

c　_____ need strong muscles in their _____

so they can fly and strong muscles in their _____ so they can run.

d　_____ need strong muscles in their

_____ so they can run.

birds

fish

insects

mammals

legs

sides

chest

wings

3 Use the names of these animals to complete the lists below.
You will need to use some names more than once.

a Which three animals move but have no legs?

_____

_____

_____

Spider

Bee

Bird

b Which three animals walk and run?

_____

_____

_____

Earthworm

c Which three animals can fly?

_____

_____

_____

Bat

Leopard

d Which two animals have soft bodies?

_____

_____

Fish

Anemone

4 Draw lines to match these sentence halves about animal movements.

a Cheetahs move very quickly and

they push through the soil.

b Earthworms create a burrow as they move because

contract, causing the body to bend from side to side.

c Sea anemones feed by

are the fastest runners of all animals.

d The muscles in the sides of a fish

catching prey in their tentacles.

Pages 54–55

Muscles

Muscles are the parts of the body that cause movement. Some muscles are attached to bones. They work in pairs so we can move these bones.

REMEMBER!
All muscles work by contracting (getting shorter) to squeeze or pull on something.

1 Think about which muscles move bones and which muscles move organs. Circle the muscles in the list below that move bones.

a upper arm

b lower leg

c thigh

d tongue

e stomach

f heart

g forearm

h hands

2 Use the key to help you color in the pairs of muscles to show which one is contracted and which one is relaxed. Then, draw arrows to show which direction the arm is moving in.

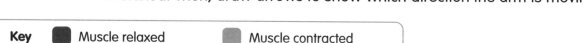

Key ■ Muscle relaxed ■ Muscle contracted

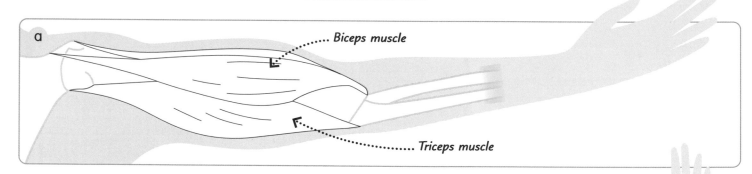

a

Biceps muscle

Triceps muscle

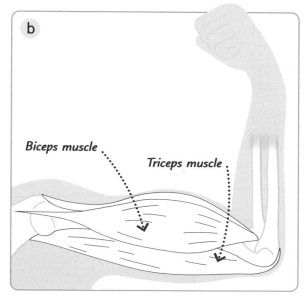

b

Biceps muscle

Triceps muscle

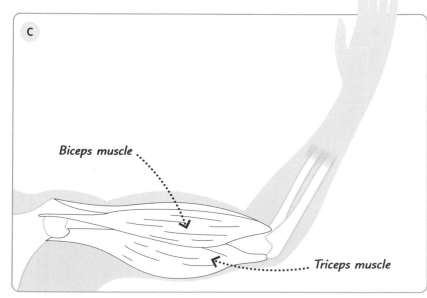

c

Biceps muscle

Triceps muscle

3 Use the words in the word box to help you label these pictures of the three types of muscle.

skeletal muscle   cardiac muscle

smooth muscle

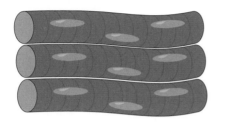

a _____   b _____   c _____

4 Read these sentence and decide whether the muscles described are voluntary or involuntary. Then, classify each of the muscle types by writing "V" if it's voluntary or "IV" if it's involuntary.

a Muscles in the stomach contract and relax to push food through the digestive system. ☐

b The heart muscle contracts and relaxes to pump blood through the circulatory system. ☐

c The muscles in the upper leg contract and relax in order to allow movement. ☐

REMEMBER!
Voluntary muscles are muscles that we control. Involuntary muscles are muscles that work automatically.

5 Draw lines to match these sentence halves about muscles.

a Skeletal muscles   keep working nonstop.

b Smooth muscles   are controlled consciously.

c Cardiac muscles   are found in the digestive system.

d Involuntary muscles   have long, slender fibers.

e Voluntary muscles   work automatically.

Pages 56–57

Skeleton

The human skeleton is made up of 206 bones of different shapes and sizes.

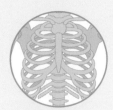

Rib bones protect the heart and lungs.

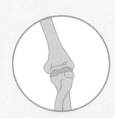

Limb bones have joints that help the body move.

Hip bones support strong muscles.

The skull protects the brain.

1 Use the words in the word box to help you label the bones on this skeleton.

| backbone | hand bones | skull | hip bones |
| foot bones | rib bones | limb bones | |

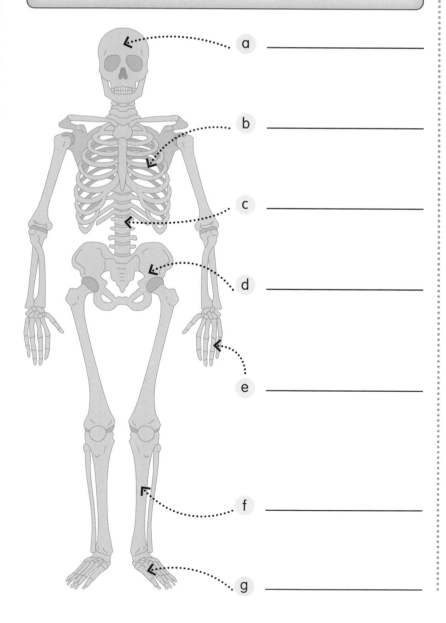

a _____

b _____

c _____

d _____

e _____

f _____

g _____

2 Look at the skeleton and then use the words from the word box in question 1 to help you complete these sentences. You will need to use some words twice.

a The _____

are shaped like a cradle.

b The _____

is shaped like a helmet.

c The _____

are shaped like a cage.

d The _____

is long and flexible.

e The _____

are small and thin.

f The _____ protect the heart.

g The _____

are long and rigid.

h The _____

are long and thin.

3 Circle six words about bones in the word search below. Use the words in the word box to help you.

hollow	curved	straight	light
hard	long	strong	

a	o	h	o	l	l	o	w
c	e	a	z	o	h	s	l
s	t	r	o	n	g	r	i
y	e	d	h	g	l	a	g
c	u	r	v	e	d	i	h
a	j	c	g	p	s	d	t
s	t	r	a	i	g	h	t

Then, use the same words to help you complete these sentences. You will need to use one of the words twice.

a All the bones in the human body are _____ .

b Bones have a _____ outside layer.

c Bones have a honeycomb pattern inside that makes them _____ .

d Bones are mainly _____ inside.

e Some bones, like the ones in the legs, are _____ and _____ .

f Other bones, like the ribs, are _____ .

DID YOU KNOW?
Our hands and feet contain more than half of all the bones in the human skeleton. There are 27 in each hand and 26 in each foot.

SCIENCE AT HOME

My skeleton

Measure your body and fill in the answers below.

Skull circumference:

_____

Hip to knee length:

_____

Knee to ankle length:

_____

Shoulder to elbow length:

_____

Elbow to wrist length:

_____

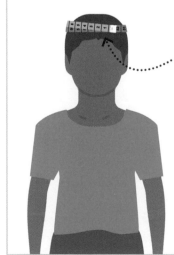

Circumference is the measurement all the way around something circular or elliptical.

Staying healthy

Staying fit and eating a balanced diet keeps your body strong, helps your bones become stronger, and helps stop you from getting sick.

> **REMEMBER!**
> When you exercise, your heart, lungs, and muscles all work harder and get stronger.

1 Exercise benefits our bodies in many ways. Use the key to help you underline these sentences in the correct color to show which body system is benefiting.

Key ⬛ Respiratory system	⬜ Circulatory system	⬜ Muscles and bones

a Bones get wider and denser.

b Muscles grow larger and stronger.

c New blood vessels form in the lungs.

d Oxygen is carried more efficiently.

e The body takes in oxygen faster.

f The heart grows larger.

2 Use the letters from question 1 to label these pictures to show how the systems in your body are strengthened by different types of exercise.

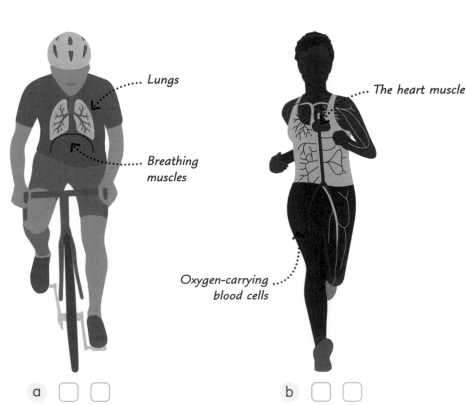

Lungs

Breathing muscles

The heart muscle

Oxygen-carrying blood cells

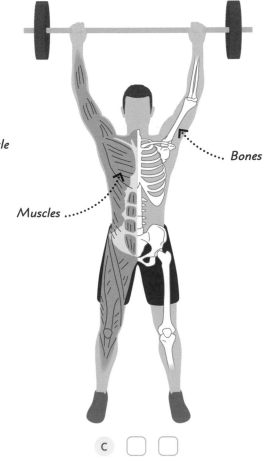

Bones

Muscles

a ☐ ☐   b ☐ ☐   c ☐ ☐

3 Read these sentences about aerobic and anaerobic exercises
   and then check the sentences that are true.

a Anaerobic exercise strengthens
   your muscles.   ☐

b Aerobic exercise includes
   weight training.   ☐

c Anaerobic exercise makes you
   get out of breath for a long time.   ☐

d Aerobic exercise benefits your
   respiratory and circulatory systems.   ☐

e Jogging is a type of aerobic exercise.   ☐

f Gymnastics doesn't strain muscles
   and bones.   ☐

4 Use these pictures to help you identify the sport that is especially good for
   each situation below. Names of sports can be used more than once.

Ball games   Sprinting

Cycling   Weight
                  training

Jogging   Gymnastics

a Strengthening bones? _____

b Improving stamina? _____

c Strengthening muscles in the lower body? _____

d Improving flexibility and balance? _____

e Putting less strain on bones and joints? _____

f Having fun and exercising together with friends? _____
   _____

SCIENCE AT HOME

My exercises

Choose an aerobic and an anaerobic activity. Then, complete these
sentences to say how the activity improves your health.

_____ is an aerobic exercise. It helps my
_____

_____ is an anaerobic exercise. It helps my
_____

📖 Pages 60–61

Animal reproduction

Adult animals can produce offspring. This is called reproduction. There are two different ways that living things reproduce: sexually and asexually.

REMEMBER!
A cloned organism is an exact genetic copy of another organism.

1 Circle the correct words or phrases to complete each of these sentences about reproduction in rabbits.

a The **male / female** sex organs are called testes.

b Females produce sex cells called **eggs / sperm**.

c **Lots of / one** sperm fertilizes an egg.

d Egg cells divide **before / after** fertilization.

e In mammals, the embryo develops **inside / outside** the female's body.

f Each offspring inherits **the same / different** characteristics.

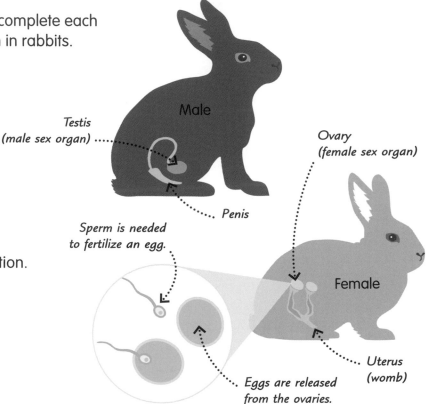

Male

Testis (male sex organ)

Penis

Sperm is needed to fertilize an egg.

Ovary (female sex organ)

Female

Eggs are released from the ovaries.

Uterus (womb)

2 Number these sentences in the correct order to explain the process of fertilization and birth.

a After an egg cell has been fertilized, it divides many times. ☐

b Males and females have sex organs. ☐

c Sperm from the male enter the female's body. ☐

d The embryo develops inside the mother's uterus. ☐

e The fertilized egg grows into an embryo. ☐

f The male and the female mate. ☐

g The sex cells join in a process called fertilization. ☐

h The sex organs produce sperm and eggs. ☐

3 Draw lines to match each kind of reproduction with the correct descriptions. There are two descriptions for each type of reproduction. One description has no match.

when there is just one parent.

| a | Sexual reproduction is |

when the offspring are all unique.

when the offspring are genetically identical to the parents.

| b | Asexual reproduction is |

when there are two parents.

when there are no parents.

4 Draw lines to match each of these images of asexual reproduction with the correct type and description below.

a

b

c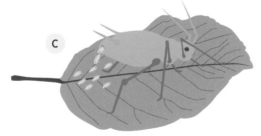

| Dividing | Fragmentation | Asexual birth |

| means dividing into fragments, which grow into whole new bodies. | means giving birth to clones, which are already pregnant with the next generation. | means splitting in two, forming identical animals with the same genes. |

Pages 62–63

Life cycle of mammals

Most mammals, including humans, spend the
first part of their life inside their mother's body.
After birth, they grow and eventually reproduce.

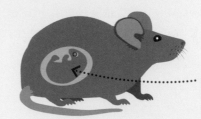

*Before birth,
a baby mammal
is called a fetus.*

1 Look at this diagram of the life cycle of a mammal. Answer the questions and
then number them to match the correct stages on the diagram.

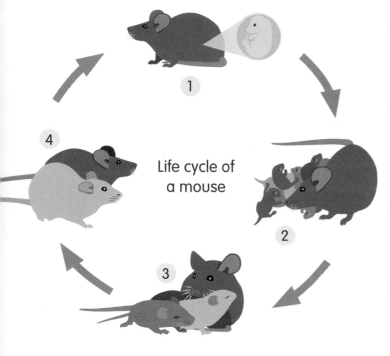

Life cycle of
a mouse

a   When can mammals reproduce?   ☐

_____

b   How do mammals learn about the
world around them?   ☐

_____

c   What do newborn mammals feed on?   ☐

_____

d   Where do baby mammals develop?   ☐

_____

2 Use the words in the word box to help you complete these
sentences about sexual reproduction in mammals.

a   Before it is born, a baby is called a _____ .

b   A group of newborn offspring is called a _____ .

c   _____ is the stage of life when a mammal can reproduce.

d   Glands on the mother's body produce _____ for the
newborn to feed on.

e   Adult animals find _____ so they can repoduce.

f   The _____ is where the fetus develops, inside the mother's body.

| uterus |
| fetus |
| litter |
| milk |
| adulthood |
| partners |

📖 Page 64

Life cycle of birds

Baby birds develop inside eggs, which are usually
laid in a nest. Most birds are looked after by their
parents in the early part of their life cycle.

1 Look at this diagram of the life cycle of a bird. Then use the
words in the word box to help you label the diagram.

> eggs   chicks
> caring for young   adult birds

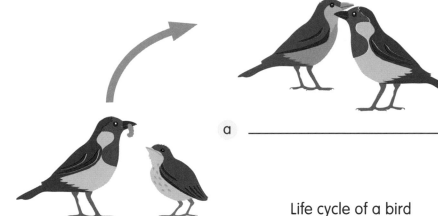

a _____

Life cycle of a bird

d _____

b _____

c _____

2 Use the words "male", "female", or "male and female" to complete these
sentences about sparrows and their young.

a _____ sparrows cooperate to build a nest.

b _____ sparrows lay eggs.

c _____ sparrows sit on the eggs to warm them.

d _____ sparrows feed their young with insects.

📖 Page 65

How eggs work

Birds develop inside eggs. An egg starts out as one huge cell. It divides over time to form the different tissues and organs of the chick.

REMEMBER!
It takes 21 days for a chick to develop fully inside its egg. Then, the chick uses its egg tooth to break out of its shell.

1 Use the words in the word box to help you complete this table about the different parts of an egg.

yolk   embryo   air sac
chalazae   white   shell

Part of egg	a _____	b _____	c _____	d _____	e _____	f _____
Position	on the outside of the egg	on top of the egg between the shell and chalazae	between the white and the yolk	in the center	inside the yolk	between the shell and the yolk
Function	lets in air	helps the chick start to breathe	holds the yolk in place	provides nourishment for the embryo	becomes the chick	protects and provides nourishment for the embryo

2 Use the words from the word box in question 1 to help you label the different parts of the egg below.

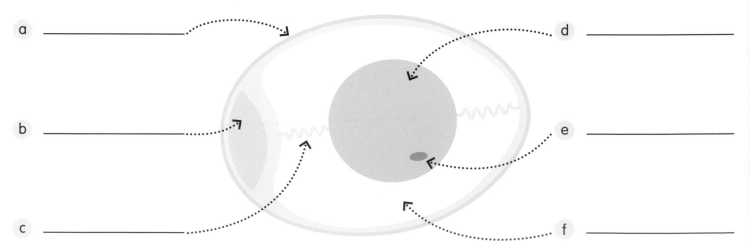

a _____

b _____

c _____

d _____

e _____

f _____

3 Use the words in the word box to help you complete these sentences about the development of a chick.

a First, the embryo's _____ start to grow.

b The _____ are developing, and the beak appears.

c The claws, nostrils, _____ , and scales grow.

d The chick chips away at the shell with its egg _____ .

e The chick takes its first _____ .

f The chick leaves the _____ .

breath
tooth
feathers
limbs
shell
wings

4 Use these diagrams to help you answer the questions below about the development of a chick.

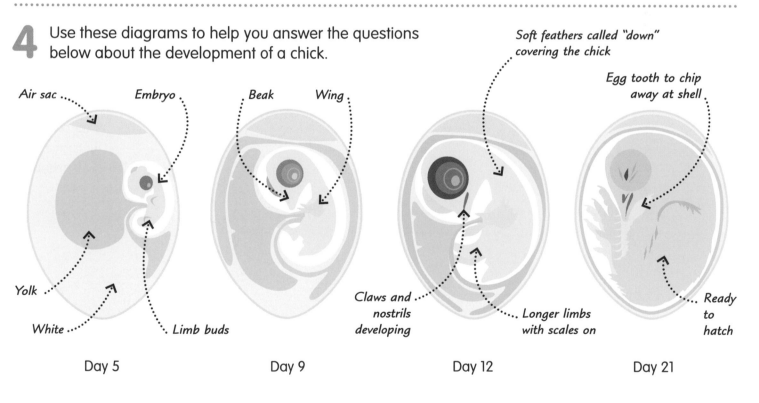

Day 5   Day 9   Day 12   Day 21

a After how many days does the chick have wings?

_____

b What new body parts does the chick have at nine days old?

_____

c When will the chick grow feathers and scales?

_____

d When will the chick hatch?

_____

Life cycle of amphibians

Frogs are part of a group of animals called amphibians. Many amphibians spend their early life in water and their adult life on land. Their bodies go through a dramatic change, called metamorphosis, as they prepare for life on land.

1 Use the words in the word box to help you label the six stages in the life cycle of a frog.

a _____

b _____

c _____

d _____

e _____

f _____

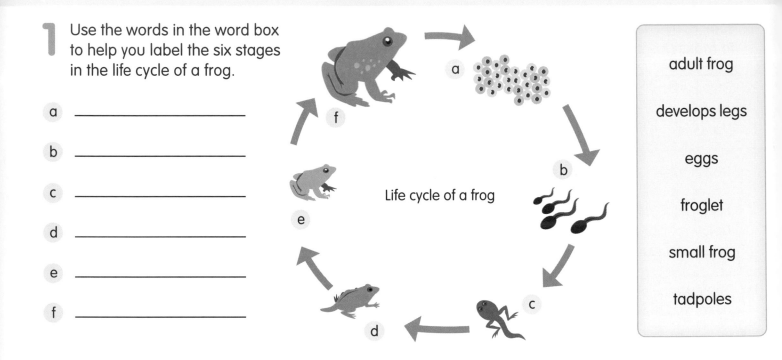

Life cycle of a frog

adult frog

develops legs

eggs

froglet

small frog

tadpoles

2 Look at the diagram of the frog's life cycle in question 1. Then check the correct columns in this table to identify the life stages at which each of these developments happens.

	Tadpole	Froglet	Adult frog
a Can breathe on land			
b Can live underwater			
c Has lungs			
d Has gills			
e Has back legs			
f Has front legs			
g Has a tail			
h Can swim			
i Can walk			

Page 68

Life cycle of insects

Many insects go through metamorphosis as they develop into adults. The change takes place during a motionless stage in the life cycle, when an insect is called a pupa.

DID YOU KNOW?
Some insects only live for a few hours when they become adults.

1 Look at this diagram of the life cycle of a butterfly. Then, read the sentences and number them to match the correct stages on the diagram. You will need to use one of the stages twice.

a The caterpillar hatches and starts feeding. ☐

b Eggs are laid on the underside of leaves. ☐

c The adult butterfly doesn't grow and only lives for a few weeks. ☐

d The caterpillar becomes a pupa. ☐

e The caterpillar eats all the time and sheds its skin to grow. ☐

f The caterpillar has a grublike body. ☐

g The pupa becomes a butterfly. ☐

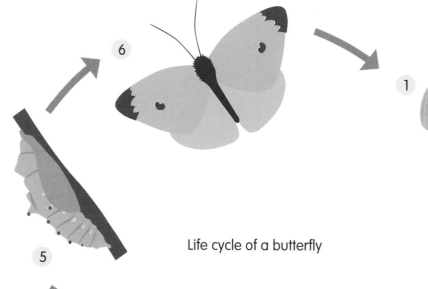

Life cycle of a butterfly

2 Circle the correct words or phrases to complete each of these sentences about insects.

a Insects **change / don't change** the way they get oxygen as they grow.

b Insects **have / don't have** a motionless stage during their life cycle.

c Caterpillars need to shed their **skin / wings** so their bodies can expand.

d In the motionless stage, an insect is called a **baby / pupa.**

📖 Page 69

Growth and development

As you get older, your body changes. The most dramatic changes happen during childhood and adolescence, but you continue changing throughout your life.

1 In this word snake, circle six words or phrases about human development. Use the words in the word box to help you. Then, use the same words to label the six stages in the pictures below.

early adulthood	old age	infancy	childhood	late adulthood	adolescence

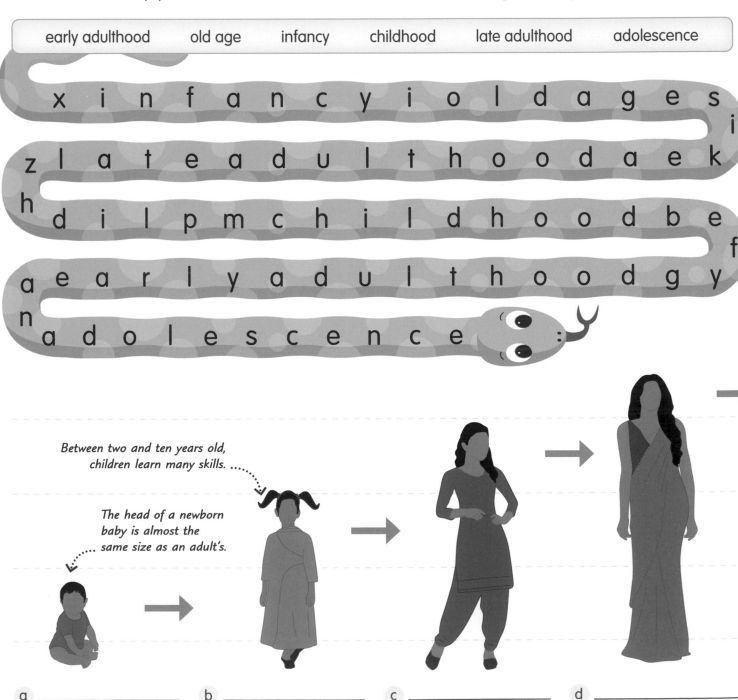

x i n f a n c y i o l d a g e s
i
z l a t e a d u l t h o o d a e k
h
d i l p m c h i l d h o o d b e
f
a e a r l y a d u l t h o o d g y
n
a d o l e s c e n c e

Between two and ten years old, children learn many skills.

The head of a newborn baby is almost the same size as an adult's.

a _____   b _____   c _____   d _____

2 Match these developmental stages to the stages from the diagram in question 1.

a Social skills such as speaking develop:

_____

b Babies grow and become stronger:

_____

c The body is prepared to have babies:

_____

d Muscles become weaker and senses may

deteriorate: _____

e Hair begins to turn gray: _____

f Bones are at their strongest:

_____

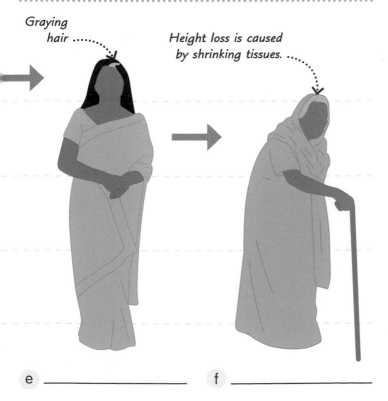

Graying hair ....

Height loss is caused by shrinking tissues. ......

e _____   f _____

3 Use the data in this growth chart to help you answer the questions below.

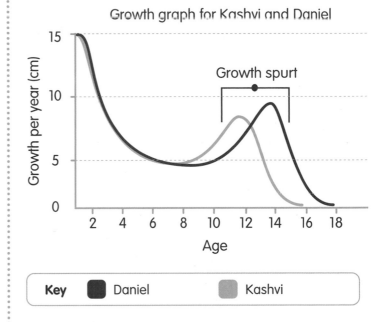

Growth graph for Kashvi and Daniel

Key	■ Daniel	■ Kashvi

a Between what ages did Kashvi have her

growth spurt? _____

b Who went through their growth spurt first?

_____

c At what age did Daniel stop growing?

_____

d Did Kashvi grow for as many years as Daniel?

_____

SCIENCE AT HOME

Write the name of someone you know at each stage shown in the pictures in question 1.

1. _____   2. _____

3. _____   4. _____

5. _____   6. _____

Evolution

Over time, living things change as they adapt to their environments, and new species are formed. This is called evolution. It is driven by a process called natural selection.

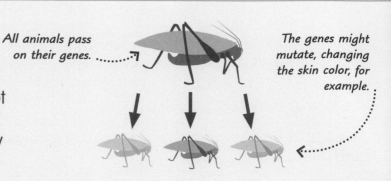

All animals pass on their genes.

The genes might mutate, changing the skin color, for example.

1 Draw lines to match these sentence halves about evolution.

a   Living organisms pass on

b   Offspring

c   The variations in genes

d   The successful offspring

sometimes have variations in their genes.

genes to the next generation.

pass on the variations to the next generation.

affect the offspring's chances of survival.

2 Which beetle do you think will have the best chance of survival in each of these environments? Fill in your answers below.

Golden beetle

Pink beetle

Green beetle

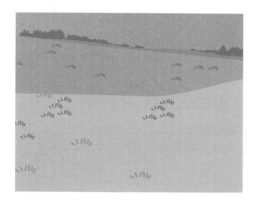

a _____ beetle   b _____ beetle   c _____ beetle

3 Check the correct columns in this table to show which body parts Archaeopteryx had and which parts a modern bird has.

Archaeopteryx

	a Archaeopteryx	b Modern bird
Teeth		
Front claws		
Back claws		
Feathers		
Bony tail		
Tail with no bones		
Wings		

Modern bird

4 Use the words in the word box to help you complete these sentences about evolution.

adapt   evolution   mutate   natural selection   survival of the fittest   variation

a When genes _____ , they change things, such as skin, eye, and hair color.

b Living organisms sometimes change because they have to _____ to a new environment.

c _____ means that only organisms that adapt will survive.

d Mutations in genes cause _____ in the offspring, such as changes in the color of hair.

e _____ is driven by a process called natural selection.

f _____ means that only those that survive and breed can pass their genes on to the next generation.

📖 Pages 82–83

Plants

Plants grow on land or in water, but they can't move from place to place.
Nearly all plants make their own food, using energy from sunlight.

1 Read these statements about plants and then circle true (T) or false (F) for each.

a   Plants make their own food.   T / F

b   Plants move slowly from place to place.   T / F

c   Leaves capture sunlight in order to make food for the plant.   T / F

d   Plants don't need air to survive.   T / F

e   Roots make the seeds that become new plants.   T / F

f   The stem carries water and nutrients to the different parts of the plant.   T / F

2 Complete this table by filling in the names for each part of the plant.

a _____	anchor the plant to the ground.
	take in water and nutrients.
b _____	captures sunlight.
	creates food.
c _____	makes seeds.
	has petals.
d _____	carries water and nutrients to the parts of the plant.

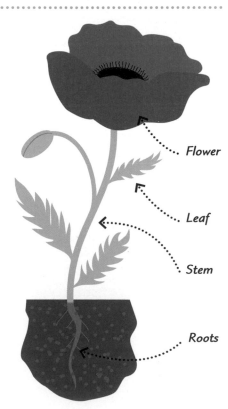

Flower

Leaf

Stem

Roots

3 Check the pictures that show the things a plant needs to survive. Then, use the picture labels to complete the information below.

a Sunlight ☐   b The right temperature ☐   c Solid food ☐   d Soil ☐

e Sugar ☐   f Air ☐   g Water ☐

h Plants make their own food by using _____ . They need _____ so they

don't wilt. Most plants get nutrients from the _____ . Plants also need carbon dioxide,

which they get from the _____ . Plants grow best when they are at _____

_____ , which varies—some plants like hot weather, but others prefer cool weather.

4 Think about the jobs that different parts of the plant do and what plants need to survive. Then, answer these questions.

a Which part of the plant absorbs minerals? _____

b Where do the minerals come from? _____

c Which part of the plant captures sunlight? _____

d Why do plants need sunlight? _____

e Which part of the plant carries water to the rest of the plant? _____

f Why do plants need water? _____

g Which part of the plant produces seeds? _____

h Why do most plants have seeds? _____

Pages 84–85

Types of plant

Plants vary from specks of green that live in water to towering trees. There are two main groups of plants: flowering and nonflowering.

DID YOU KNOW?
Scientists have identified more than 400,000 different species (types) of plants.

1 Draw arrows to show the stages of the life cycle of flowering plants. Then, use the words in the word box to help you label the three stages.

flower

seedling

new seeds

Bright colors and sugar-rich nectar attract insects.

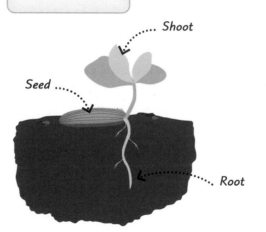

Shoot

Seed

Root

a _____

b _____

Feathery parachutes help dandelion seeds fly away on the wind.

c _____

2 Read these sentences about the life cycle of flowering plants. Then, use the letters from question 1 to match these activities to the correct stages of the life cycle.

a   Seeds absorb water. ☐

b   A baby plant is formed. ☐

c   Pollinated flowers produce new seeds. ☐

d   Brightly colored flowers attract insects. ☐

e   Animals carry sex cells from flower to flower. ☐

f   Some seeds have wings to catch the wind. ☐

3 Draw lines to match each nonflowering plant with the correct description.

 a Mosses

 b Algae

 c Ferns

 d Conifers

| have delicate leaves and live in shady places. | can be huge trees. | live in water. | are small plants that grow in damp places. |

4 Use the words in the word box to help you complete each of these statements about nonflowering plants.

conifers   mosses   ferns   algae

a _____ make spores.

b _____ are microscopic.

c _____ have no roots.

d _____ have no flowers.

e _____ have seeds inside cones.

f _____ have no seeds.

g _____ live in water.

h _____ have no stems.

SCIENCE AT HOME

Plant list

1. Ask an adult to help you find out the names of some of the plants in your home, garden, or local park.

2. Write the plant names in the correct category below.

Flowering plants

Nonflowering plants

Pages 86–87

Flowers

Flowers can be many shapes, sizes, and colors.
They produce the male and female cells that
allow plants to reproduce sexually.

> **REMEMBER!**
> Not all plants reproduce
> by making flowers.

1 Use the words in the word boxes to help you label this picture of a flower.

Female parts:

> stigma　　carpel　　ovary

Male parts:

> stamen　　pollen

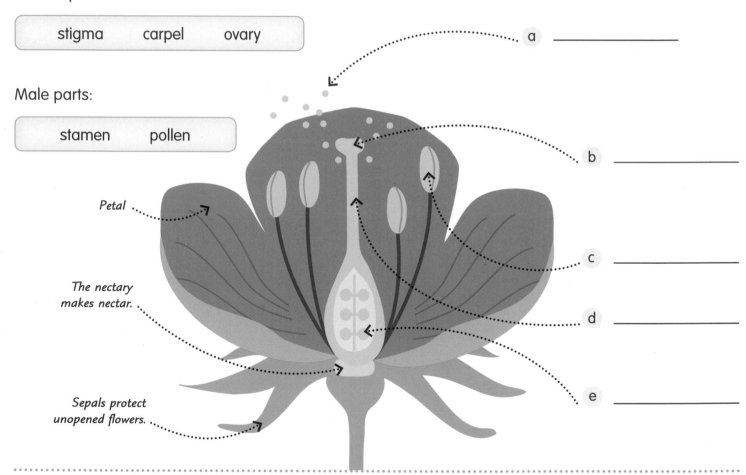

Petal

The nectary
makes nectar.

Sepals protect
unopened flowers.

a _____

b _____

c _____

d _____

e _____

2 Some flowers need to attract insects so that the insects can pollinate
them. Check three features below that help flowers attract insects.

a Long stems ☐

b Interesting names ☐

c Colorful petals ☐

d Sweet nectar ☐

e Sweet scent ☐

f Lots of roots ☐

3 Look at this diagram showing the process of pollination. Then, read the sentences and number them to match the correct stages on the diagram.

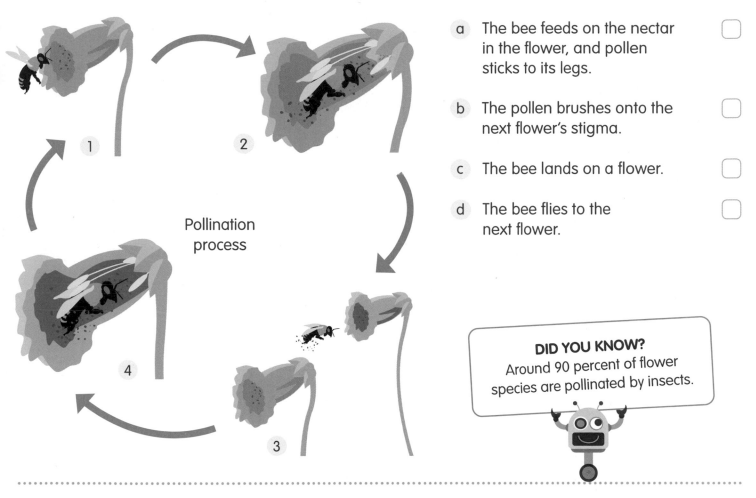

Pollination process

a   The bee feeds on the nectar in the flower, and pollen sticks to its legs. ☐

b   The pollen brushes onto the next flower's stigma. ☐

c   The bee lands on a flower. ☐

d   The bee flies to the next flower. ☐

DID YOU KNOW?
Around 90 percent of flower species are pollinated by insects.

4 Circle the correct words to complete each of these sentences about flowers.

a   The **petals / stamen / ovary** of the flower becomes the fruit.

b   The **seeds / stamen / ovary** of the flower falls off.

c   The male cells fertilize the female cells to make **seeds / fruit / flowers**.

d   The **stigma / stamen / ovary** is at the top of the carpel.

e   Bees carry male **scent / nectar / sex cells** between plants.

f   Pollination is necessary for plants to produce **roots / fruit / leaves**.

g   Animals swallow the fruit and carry the **stamen / fruit / seeds** to a new place.

📖 Pages 92–93

Seed dispersal

Seeds must be scattered, or dispersed, far
from the parent plant in order to grow and thrive.
They can be scattered in several different ways.

DID YOU KNOW?
The largest seed in the world is
produced by a palm tree, the
coco de mer. It can be 50 cm
long and weighs up to 25 kg.

1 Use the words "animal", "wind", or "water" to label these pictures showing
the three main types of seed dispersal.

a _____

b _____

c _____

d _____

e _____

f _____

g _____

h _____

2 Use the pictures in question 1 to help you answer these questions
about animals that spread seeds.

Which animal disperses seeds by:

a   eating the fruit and pooping out the seeds? _____

b   burying them and then forgetting about them? _____

c   carrying the seeds away from the plant, stuck to their fur? _____

3 Fill in the names of the plants that match each of the descriptions below.

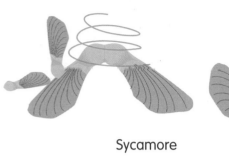

Sycamore

Dandelion

Pea

Poppy

a These seeds are shaped like wings. They spin round and fall to the ground: _____

b These seeds explode out of the pod: _____

c These seeds are very light and float in the wind: _____

d These seeds are shaken out of the dried seed head: _____

4 Circle the correct words or phrases to complete each of these sentences about seeds.

a Floating seeds are usually **smaller / larger** than flying seeds.

b Exploding seeds **can / can't** travel far when there is no wind.

c Seeds that travel on the sea usually travel **farther / less far** than seeds that hitch a ride on animals.

d Plants with seeds that fly usually produce **more / fewer** seeds than plants with seeds that float.

e **Some / all** of the seeds hoarded by animals grow into new plants.

f Seeds that travel on the wind are usually **smaller / larger** than seeds that float in water.

📖 Pages 94–95

How seeds grow

Germination is when seeds sprout and grow into new plants. Some seeds can survive for centuries before germinating.

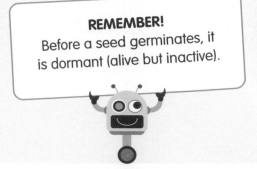

REMEMBER!
Before a seed germinates, it is dormant (alive but inactive).

1 Look at this diagram of a seed, then use the labels to complete the sentences below.

A seed has a tough _____ as protection.

Inside the seed, there is a tiny baby plant called an

_____ , which has a _____ , a _____ ,

and the _____ . There are also seed leaves inside

the seed that are a _____ for the plant.

Shoot ··········   ·········· *Embryo*

Root ··········   ········· *First true leaves*

·········· *Seed leaves (food store)*

·········· *Outer coat*

2 Number these sentences to match the correct stages in the picture below showing how seeds grow. There are two sentences for each stage.

a   The true leaves will make food for the plant. ☐

b   The seed leaves supply the plant with food. ☐

c   Tiny hairs on the roots absorb water and minerals from the soil. ☐

d   The small seedling grows its first true leaves. ☐

e   The outer coat of the seed cracks, and a small root grows. ☐

f   The plant's first shoot breaks through the soil. ☐

g   The roots of the tiny seedling grow downwards. ☐

h   The seed's growth is fueled by its food store. ☐

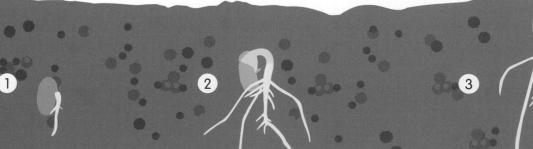

3 These pictures show six seeds that have fallen on the ground. Check three places where the seeds are unlikely to germinate and explain why by completing the sentences below.

1 ☐  2 ☐  3 ☐  4 ☐  5 ☐  6 ☐

a Place ____ is bad for germination because there isn't _____

b Place ____ is bad for germination because there isn't _____

c Place ____ is bad for germination because there isn't _____

REMEMBER!
Plants produce a lot of seeds because only the ones that fall in the right places will grow.

SCIENCE AT HOME

Starting seeds

Choose two rooms in your house that have the best conditions for seed germination and complete this information for each of them.

Room 1: _____

Position in the room: _____

Why is this place good for germinating seeds?

_____

Room 2: _____

Position in the room: _____

Why is this place good for germinating seeds?

_____

4

📖 Pages 96–97

Asexual reproduction in plants

In asexual reproduction, there is only one parent.
Many plants reproduce asexually, which allows
them to multiply in number and spread quickly.

1 In this word snake, circle eight words or phrases about asexual reproduction in plants. Use the
words in the word box to help you. Then, use the same words to label the pictures below.

| rhizome | runner | corm | sucker | asexual seeds | tuber | bulb | plantlet |

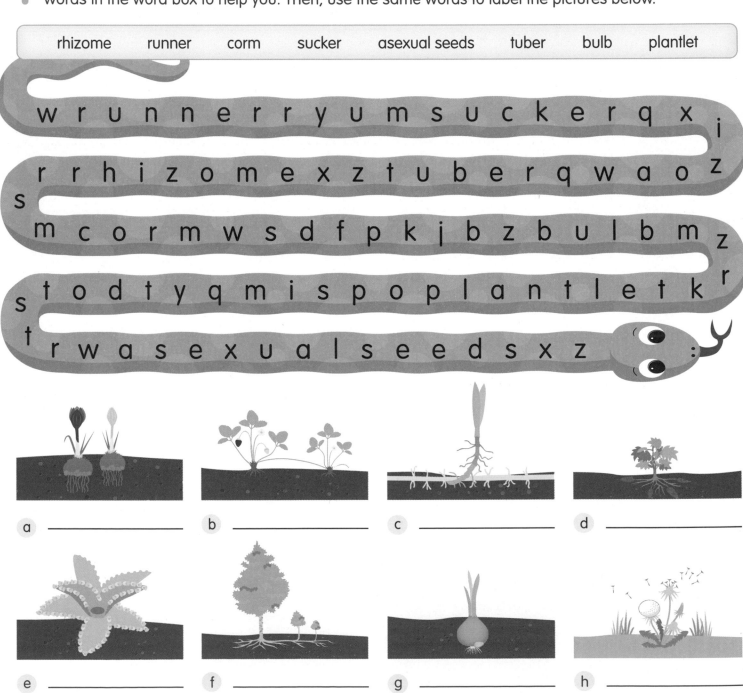

w r u n n e r r y u m s u c k e r q x i

r r h i z o m e x z t u b e r q w a o z

s m c o r m w s d f p k j b z b u l b m z

t o d t y q m i s p o p l a n t l e t k r

s t r w a s e x u a l s e e d s x z :

a _____

b _____

c _____

d _____

e _____

f _____

g _____

h _____

2 Use the words from the word box in question 1 to complete these sentences about types of reproduction.

a   Stem that grows horizontally
    underground: _____

b   Underground swelling that produces
    buds: _____

c   A round food store that forms from
    a stem and has buds: _____

d   Seeds that are clones of the parent
    plant: _____

e   Horizontal stem that takes root and
    forms new plants: _____

f   Sideways root with buds that form
    new trees: _____

g   Underground food store with bulblets
    around the base: _____

h   Tiny growths on the edge of leaves
    that form new plants: _____

3 Use the words "cutting" and "grafting" to label these pictures. Then, number each set of sentences below to show the order in which these processes happen.

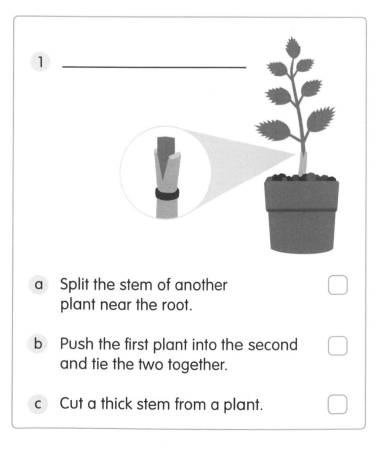

1   _____

a   Split the stem of another
    plant near the root. ☐

b   Push the first plant into the second
    and tie the two together. ☐

c   Cut a thick stem from a plant. ☐

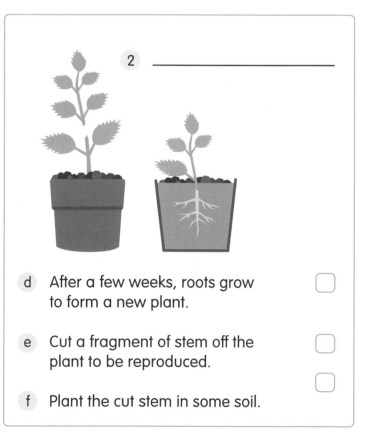

2   _____

d   After a few weeks, roots grow
    to form a new plant. ☐

e   Cut a fragment of stem off the
    plant to be reproduced. ☐

    ☐

f   Plant the cut stem in some soil.

Single-celled organisms

Unlike animals and plants, single-celled organisms are made of only one cell. The world is full of them, and they live everywhere.

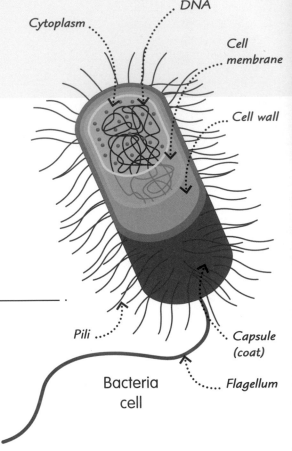

Cytoplasm

DNA

Cell membrane

Cell wall

Pili

Capsule (coat)

Flagellum

Bacteria cell

1 Look at this diagram of a bacteria cell and then use the labels to complete the sentences below.

a   Some bacteria have a long tail called a _____ .

This tail rotates to make the bacteria move.

b   Lots of bacteria are protected by a _____ ,

which is sometimes covered in small hairs called _____ .

c   The bacteria's genes are carried in the _____ ,

which is in the _____ .

d   This is protected by a _____ membrane

and a _____ wall.

2 Use the words in the word box to help you complete this table about types of algae.

Chlamydomonas   chlorella   diatom

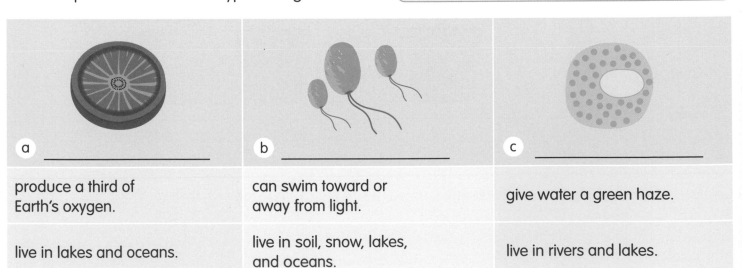

a _____	b _____	c _____
produce a third of Earth's oxygen.	can swim toward or away from light.	give water a green haze.
live in lakes and oceans.	live in soil, snow, lakes, and oceans.	live in rivers and lakes.

3 Look at these pictures of how an amoeba feeds and then draw lines to match each picture with the correct descriptions. There are two descriptions for each picture.

REMEMBER!
Amoebas are a kind of protozoa. These are a diverse group of single-celled organisms that mostly feed on other single-celled organisms.

1	2	3
The pseudopods join and enclose their prey.	The amoeba detects prey.	Pseudopods reach around the prey to trap it.

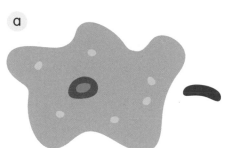

b

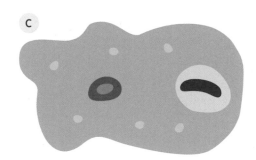

c

4	5	6
The contents of the cells flow into the pseudopods.	Digestive juices digest the prey.	The amoeba follows its prey.

4 Read these sentences about how bacteria are used to clean dirty water. Cross out the words that are wrong and then write the correct word at the end of each sentence. The first one has been done for you.

a **Step 1:** ~~Clean~~ water is trickled onto ponds full of gravel particles.   _Dirty_

b **Step 2:** Moss grows as a slimy film on the gravel particles.   _____

c **Step 3:** Organic matter in the soil feeds the bacteria.   _____

d **Step 4:** The bacteria kill and digest the harmful fish.   _____

e **Step 5:** Salty water flows out from the bottom.   _____

📖 Pages 100–101

Food chains and recycling

Food chains show us how energy flows through an ecosystem. Energy in the food is passed along the food chain from one organism to another.

REMEMBER!
The biomass pyramid shows the total weight of all organisms at each level.

1 Use the words in the word box to help you label this diagram of a food chain.

decomposers	energy source	primary consumers	producers
secondary consumers		tertiary consumers	

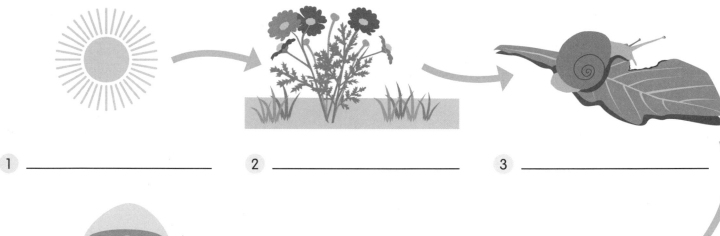

1 _____

2 _____

3 _____

6 _____

5 _____

4 _____

2 Number these sentences to match the pictures they describe in question 1.

a Animals that eat producers ☐

b Animals that prey on secondary consumers ☐

c Animals that digest dead organisms ☐

d Organisms that make their own food ☐

e The energy for the food chain ☐

f Animals that eat primary consumers ☐

3 Read these sentences about consumers and producers in a food chain and then circle true (T) or false (F) for each.

In a food chain:

a Consumers are always bigger   T / F   b Producers are organisms that   T / F
   than producers.   create their own food.

c Decomposers make their   T / F   d There are more tertiary consumers   T / F
   own food.   than primary consumers.

e There are more primary consumers   T / F   f The energy source is different for   T / F
   than secondary consumers.   producers and consumers.

4 Look at this a biomass pyramid for an ocean food chain and then number the organisms to match the correct levels in the pyramid.

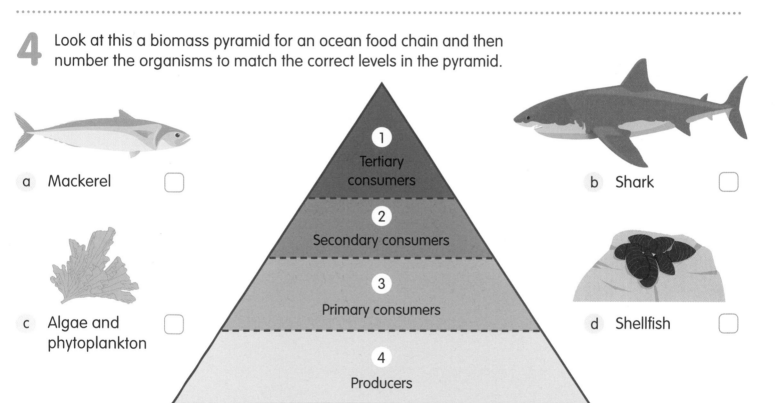

a Mackerel ☐

c Algae and phytoplankton ☐

1 Tertiary consumers
2 Secondary consumers
3 Primary consumers
4 Producers

b Shark ☐

d Shellfish ☐

5 Circle the correct words to complete each of these sentences about biomass pyramids.

a **Most / Some** of the energy escapes as it passes through the food chain.

b The amount of energy available **increases / decreases** as it passes along the food chain.

c The total weight of biomass as we move up the pyramid becomes **smaller / bigger**.

d There are **more / fewer** producers than primary consumers.

Humans and the environment

Earth's human population has quadrupled in the last hundred years. Supplying the growing population with energy and other resources can harm the natural environment in many ways.

1 Use the words in the word box to help you label these pictures of threats to the environment. Then, draw lines to match each picture with the correct description.

habitat loss	pollution	overexploitation	invasive species

a _____

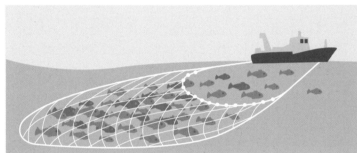

b _____

Habitats are cleared to make room for human needs.	Animals are caught faster than they can reproduce.	New species replace native species.	Some chemicals build up to toxic levels in the food chain.

c _____

d _____

2 Read these sets of sentences about two different threats to our environment. Number each set in the correct order and then identify the threat it describes.

a The animal escapes. ☐

It has no natural predators. ☐

It replaces the native species. ☐

Someone brings a nonnative animal into the country. ☐

Type of threat: _____

b Their numbers decline dangerously. ☐

An animal species is hunted. ☐

They become extinct. ☐

The species cannot multiply fast enough. ☐

Type of threat: _____

3 Underline five sentences about ways in which biodiversity benefits humans and the environment.

a Wild plants can be used to develop new varieties of crops for food.

b Biodiversity increases the amount of maize we can produce.

c Plant-rich ecosystems reduce flooding.

d Many medicines originally come from plants.

e Rain forests can be cut down to make cattle ranches.

f We need lots of insects to pollinate food crops.

> **REMEMBER!**
> An ecosystem that has many different animals and plants has a high biodiversity.

4 Answer these questions about biodiversity.

a Which three plant species provide 60 percent of the world's food?

_____

_____

_____

_____

b How can plants in the rain forest help us fight disease?

_____

_____

_____

_____

c Why is it important to develop new varieties of crops?

_____

_____

_____

_____

📖 Pages 106–107

States of matter

Most substances exist in three different forms:
solid, liquid, or gas. These three states of matter exist
because molecules can pack together in different ways.

REMEMBER!
Solids have a definite shape
and volume, liquids have a
definite volume, but gases have
no definite shape or volume.

1 Look at these diagrams of molecules and then use the words
in the word box to help you complete the sentences below.

| liquid | solid | gas |

 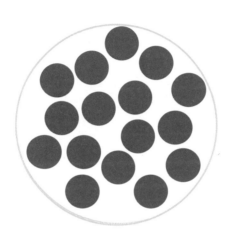 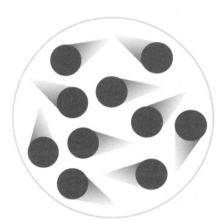

a In a _____ , the
molecules are packed
together very tightly. They
cannot move around easily.

b In a _____ , the
molecules slide past each
other. They can move
around quite easily.

c In a _____ , the
molecules can spread out
in all directions. They can
move around very easily.

2 Substances exist in different states of matter in the world around us. Circle the
correct state of matter for each of the examples below.

a Wood

solid / liquid / gas

b Paint

solid / liquid / gas

c Spoon

solid / liquid / gas

d Smoke

solid / liquid / gas

3 Circle six words about the states of matter in the word search below. Use the words in the word box to help you.

oxygen	milk
fork	toothbrush
smoke	honey

g	u	f	w	a	n	e	x	b	o
c	u	o	b	r	a	y	s	u	x
v	z	r	m	i	l	k	m	r	y
f	q	k	e	p	o	l	o	u	g
v	k	f	i	q	r	c	k	i	e
r	h	o	n	e	y	r	e	e	n
t	o	o	t	h	b	r	u	s	h

4 Classify the words from the word box in question 3 by writing them into the correct columns in the table below.

a Solid	b Liquid	c Gas

5 The way the molecules are packed together in solids, liquids, and gases gives them special properties. Draw lines to match each state of matter with the correct description.

| a Solids | b Liquids | c Gases |

| can be poured and have no fixed shape. | have no fixed shape and fill the whole container. | have a fixed shape. |

Pages 112–113

Changing state

When solids melt or liquids freeze, we say they've changed state. Each time a substance changes state, it loses or gains energy.

When a substance changes state, it is still the same chemical. Ice, liquid water, and steam are all forms of water.

1 Use the words in the word box to help you label this diagram showing the changing states of matter.

| liquid | evaporation | solid | condensation | gas | freezing | melting |

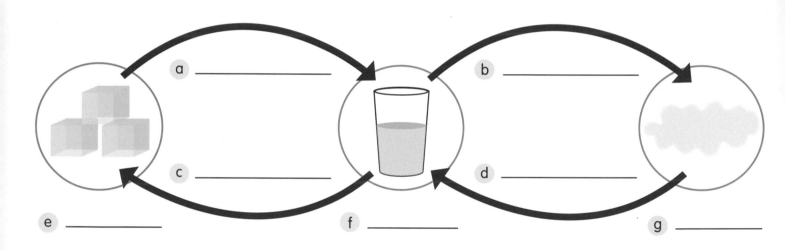

a _____
b _____
c _____
d _____
e _____
f _____
g _____

2 Substances change state when they are heated or cooled. Use the words in the word box to help you complete these sentences about freezing and melting.

REMEMBER!
Freezing and melting happen when substances are cooled or heated, making their molecules move.

a _____ is when molecules lose energy, which makes them move very close together.

b _____ is when molecules gain energy, which makes them move farther apart from each other.

c _____ is when the molecules in a liquid gain more energy, which makes them move even farther apart from each other.

d _____ is when the molecules in a gas lose energy, which makes them move closer together.

melting

condensation

freezing

evaporation

3 Draw lines to match each picture with the correct change of state below.

a Freezing   b Melting   c Evaporation   d Condensation

| solid → liquid | liquid → solid | gas → liquid | liquid → gas |

4 Read these sentences about changing states of matter and then circle true (T) or false (F) for each.

a When a substance changes state, it becomes a different chemical.   T / F

b Most substances change state when their temperature is changed.   T / F

c Water freezes at 0°C.   T / F

d When we cool a substance, we add energy to it.   T / F

e When molecules lose energy, they move closer together.   T / F

📖 Pages 114–115

Properties of matter

Different materials have different properties. The properties of a material determine what we use it for.

REMEMBER!
We use the Mohs scale to measure the hardness of different materials.

1 Use the words in the word box to help you complete this table about the properties of materials.

| strong | brittle | ductile | elastic | flexible | hard | malleable |

a	can be stretched and squeezed, returns to its original shape
b	resists force that pushes or pulls, is able to hold weight
c	can be beaten or pressed into a different shape, can be rolled out thinly
d	can be stretched into a very thin wire
e	can be bent, bounces when pressed
f	doesn't bend, stretch, or change shape; breaks when force is exerted on it
g	is difficult to scratch

2 Use some of the words from the word box in question 1 to help you describe the materials these objects are made of. The first one has been done for you.

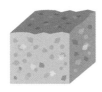

a   Concrete: _____hard_____

b   Glass: _____

c   Rubber band: _____

d   Soft clay: _____

e   Copper wire: _____

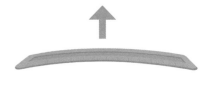

f   Plastic ruler: _____

3 Look at the Mohs scale below and then draw lines to match these sentence halves about materials and their hardness.

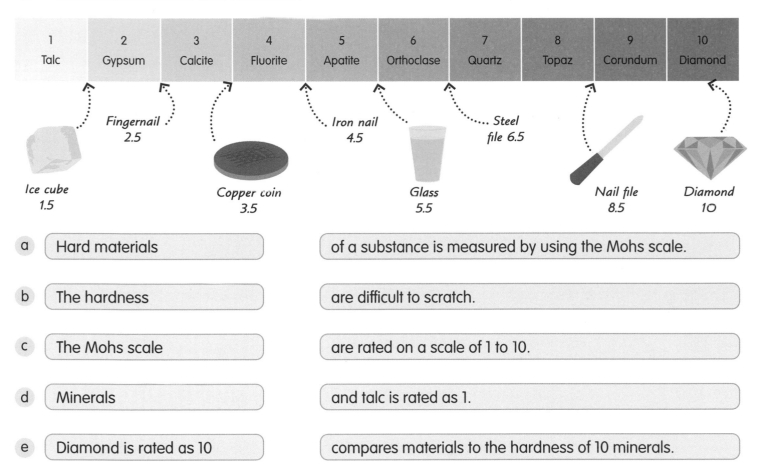

a Hard materials   of a substance is measured by using the Mohs scale.

b The hardness   are difficult to scratch.

c The Mohs scale   are rated on a scale of 1 to 10.

d Minerals   and talc is rated as 1.

e Diamond is rated as 10   compares materials to the hardness of 10 minerals.

4 Look at these objects and think about the materials they are made of, their properties, and how those properties change. Then, identify the material described in each sentence below.

Aluminum   Clay   Glass   Leather

a A material that is malleable but becomes brittle when heated: _____

b A metal that is malleable: _____

c A material that is both hard and brittle: _____

d A material that is both strong and malleable: _____

Pages 116–117

Expanding gases

Gases are made up of billions of atoms or molecules that move about freely. The hotter a gas gets, the faster these particles move, and the farther they spread out, making the gas expand.

REMEMBER!
Hot air rises above cold air because it is less dense. Cold air sinks below hot air because it is denser.

1 Number these sentences in the correct order to show how a hot air balloon rises and falls.

a   The balloon is on the ground because the air molecules inside and outside the balloon have the same density. ☐

b   Hot air is released from the top of the balloon and cool air is drawn in, so the air inside the balloon becomes denser, and the balloon falls. ☐

c   The warmer the air becomes inside the balloon, the less dense it gets, and so the more it rises. ☐

d   The air in the balloon is heated and becomes less dense, so the balloon starts to rise. ☐

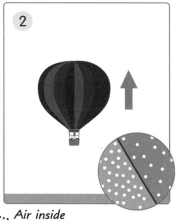
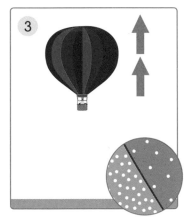
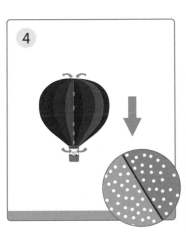

Air outside the balloon

Air inside the balloon

2 Circle the correct words or phrases to complete each of these sentences about what happens when gas expands or contracts.

a   When the molecules in air spread out, the air becomes **denser / less dense**.

b   To make air sink, we need to make it **denser / less dense**.

c   Warm air **rises / falls**.

d   When the air is less dense, it is **warmer / cooler**.

e   To make air denser, we need to **cool / heat** it.

f   As air cools, the molecules are drawn **closer together / farther apart**.

3 Look at these diagrams showing how thermal columns form and then answer the questions below.

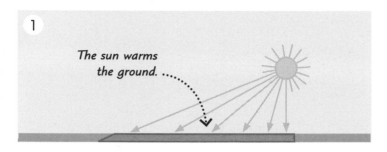

1 — The sun warms the ground.

2 — The ground warms the air above it.

3 — Warm air rises.

4 — Cool air sinks back to the ground.

a Which energy source heats the ground?

_____

b How does the air above the ground get warm?

_____

_____

c What does the air do as it warms up?

_____

d Why does the warm air rise above the cooler air?

_____

_____

e What happens to the air as it cools when it rises?

_____

_____

f How do birds use thermal columns?

_____

_____

SCIENCE AT HOME

Expanding air experiment

You will need: a balloon, an empty bottle, and two tubs of water—one with cold water and ice and the other with very warm water (ask an adult to help you with this).

1. Put the balloon over the mouth of the bottle. What is inside the bottle and the balloon?

_____

2. Stand the bottle in the tub of warm water. What happens?

_____

3. Stand the bottle in the tub of cold water. What happens?

_____

4. What does this tell you about hot and cold air?

_____

📖 Pages 118–119

Mixtures

A mixture contains different chemicals mixed together. Solids, liquids, and gases can mix together in lots of different ways.

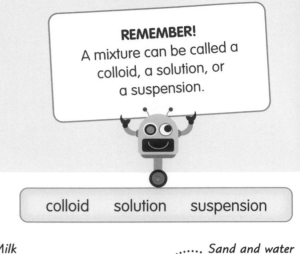

REMEMBER!
A mixture can be called a colloid, a solution, or a suspension.

| colloid | solution | suspension |

1 Use the words in the word box to help you label these mixtures. Then use the label numbers to classify the descriptions below.

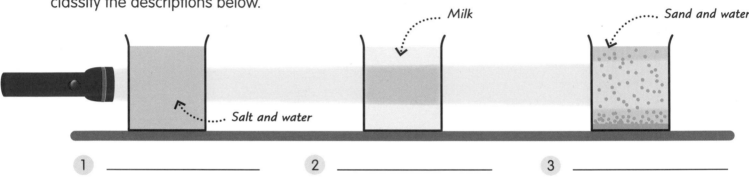

····· Milk

····· Sand and water

····· Salt and water

1 _____   2 _____   3 _____

a The mixture is completely clear and transparent. ☐

b The particles are so small that you can never see them. ☐

c The particles are big enough to scatter light. ☐

d The particles settle on the bottom of the mixture. ☐

e The particles are very large. ☐

f The beam of a flashlight shows in the mixture. ☐

2 Use the words in the word box to help you complete this table about colloids. Then, add an example for each one.

| gel | foam | aerosol | emulsion |

Name of colloid:	a _____	b _____	c _____	d _____
Mixture of:	Liquid droplets dispersed in a solid	Liquid droplets dispersed in a liquid	Liquid droplets dispersed in a gas	Gas bubbles dispersed in a solid or liquid
Example:	e _____	f _____	g _____	h _____

3

Draw lines to match each substance with the correct type of mixture.

a
Distilled
water

b
Iron
sulfide

c
Iron filings
and sulfur

d
Brass

e
Salt and
pepper

f
Bronze

| compound | mixture | alloy | pure chemical |

4

Answer these questions about the differences between an iron
and sulfur mixture and an iron sulfide compound.

······· *Mixture of iron*
filings and sulfur

······· *Iron sulfide*
compound

a How do you mix the iron filings
and sulfur?

_____

b Is there a chemical reaction?

_____

c Are the atoms chemically bonded?

_____

d Can you separate the components
with a magnet?

_____

e Is the end product a mixture or a compound?

_____

f How do the iron and sulfur form
a compound?

_____

g Is there a chemical reaction?

_____

h Are the atoms chemically bonded?

_____

i Can you separate the components
with a magnet?

_____

j Is the result a mixture or a compound?

_____

Pages 122–123

Solutions

When you stir sugar into water, it seems to vanish.
When a substance mixes evenly with a liquid in this way,
we say it dissolves. The resulting mixture is called a solution.

REMEMBER!
A substance that dissolves in a liquid is called a solute, and the liquid that it dissolves in is called a solvent.

1 Look at this picture of two beakers and then circle the correct words or phrases to complete each of these sentences about solutions.

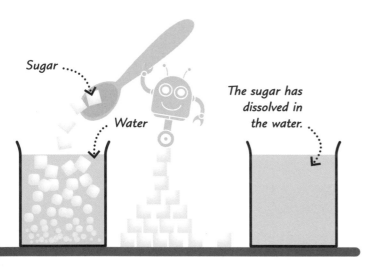

Sugar

Water

The sugar has dissolved in the water.

a The sugar cubes are the **solvent / solute**.

b The water is the **solvent / solute**.

c When a **solid / liquid** dissolves in water, its molecules **spread out / clump together**.

d When a solid dissolves in water, it becomes **visible / invisible**.

e **All / some** substances dissolve in water.

f Most things that don't dissolve in water settle on the **top / bottom** of the beaker.

2 Answer these questions about solutions.

a What word do we use to describe a solution when no more solute can be dissolved in the solvent?

_____

b What do we call a solution with only a small amount of solute in it?

_____

c Why do solutes dissolve more quickly in hot solvents?

_____

d Why do we stir a hot drink after we put sugar in it?

_____

3 Circle the pictures that show solutions.

a Oil and vinegar

b Salt water

c Fresh orange juice

d Black coffee

e Water and sand

f Vegetable soup

g Water and soil

h Fizzy lemonade

4 Number these sentences in the correct order to explain how water is carbonated.

a When you open the bottle, the pressure is released. ☐

b Carbon dioxide is dissolved in the water. ☐

c The bottle is sealed, and the contents are under pressure. ☐

d The carbon dioxide leaves the solution in the form of bubbles, making the water fizzy. ☐

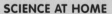

SCIENCE AT HOME

How fast?

You will need four different types of transparent liquids (such as water, fizzy water, lemonade, and apple juice), salt, sugar, a teaspoon, eight transparent cups, and a marker.

1. Label four cups with the name of one liquid each and the word "salt." Label the other four cups with the name of one liquid each and the word "sugar."

2. Add 200 ml of each liquid into each of the eight cups.

3. Add two teaspoons of sugar to each sugar cup and two teaspoons of salt to each salt cup. Let them dissolve.

4. Watch carefully and write down how long it takes for the sugar and the salt to dissolve in each liquid.

Which solvent worked the fastest?

_____

Which solute dissolved the fastest?

_____

📖 Pages 124–125

Separating mixtures 1

The chemicals in a mixture can be separated.
Sieving, decanting, and filtering are three simple
ways of separating mixtures.

DID YOU KNOW?
You can separate the salt from
salt water by letting the water dry out.

1 Look at these pictures of three different ways of separating mixtures. Then choose which method
you would use to separate each of the mixtures listed below and describe how you would do it.

Sieve ......⌐

⌐···· The rocks don't fit
through the holes.

⌐··· Sand falls
through.

Sieving

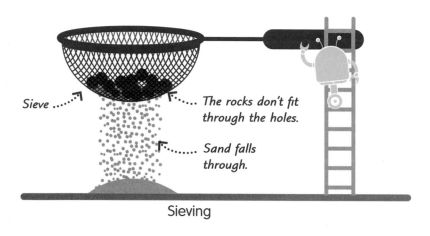

Beaker ⌐

··· Sand settles on the bottom.

⌐··· Sand is left in
the beaker.

··· Decanted
water

Decanting

The ground coffee can't pass
through the filter paper. ·····

Filter paper ·····

⌐···· Jug

⌐··· Funnel

······ Filtered coffee

Filtering

a Mixture of peas and gravy

Method: _____

I can separate this mixture by

_____

_____

b Mixture of oil and water

Method: _____

I can separate this mixture by

_____

_____

c Mixture of sugar and nuts

Method: _____

I can separate this mixture by

_____

_____

2 Use the words "beaker," "sieve," or "filter" to complete the sentences below. Then, identify which separation method is described in each sentence.

a Place the mixture of two solid substances in a _____ . Shake it until one of the

solids has fallen through the holes and the other solid substance is left in the _____ .

Separation method: _____

b Place the mixture of two liquids with different densities in a _____

Leave it until one of the mixtures rises above the other.

Separation method: _____

c Pour the mixture of insoluble particles in a liquid through a _____ .

The solid particles are left in the _____ .

Separation method: _____

3 Read these sentences about filtering, sieving, and decanting and then circle true (T) or false (F) for each.

a You can only filter insoluble solid particles from liquids.   T / F

b Filtering does not separate a cup of coffee into coffee and water.   T / F

c You can separate coffee beans from ground coffee by sieving.   T / F

d You can decant soluble and insoluble solids in mixtures.   T / F

e Sieving is used to separate two liquids.   T / F

SCIENCE AT HOME

Separating mixtures at home

You will need: sand, water, a paper coffee filter, a sieve, and some glasses.

1. Mix some sand and water in a glass. Stir well and wait for the sand to settle on the bottom of the glass. How long does it take for the sand to settle?

_____

2. Pour the sand and water mixture into another glass through the sieve. Does the water look completely clear?

_____

3. Make the sand and water mixture again and slowly decant it into another glass. Can you remove all the water this way without taking any sand?

_____

4. Finally, pour the mixture through the paper coffee filter into another glass. Is the water completely clear now?

_____

Pages 126–127

Separating mixtures 2

Like mixtures, solutions can be separated.
Evaporation and distillation are two ways
of separating solutions.

REMEMBER!
We can use heat to separate
mixtures in different ways.

1 Use the words in the word box to help you complete these sentences
about evaporation. You will need to use some words more than once.

Copper
sulfate
solution

The water
escapes
as gas.

Only solid
copper sulfate
is left.

1   Heating   2   Evaporation   3   Solid residue

copper sulfate

evaporates

gas   solid

water

a   Copper sulfate solution is a solution of _____ and _____ .

b   We heat the solution so the _____ will boil.

c   The boiling water escapes as _____ , and solid particles start to form.

d   All the water _____ .

e   Only _____ particles remain.

2 Draw lines to match each type of separation process with the correct descriptions. There are
three descriptions for each process. One description is used twice.

we heat the solution to separate the chemicals.

a   In evaporation,

we heat and cool the solution to separate the chemicals.

the water escapes as gas.

b   In distillation,

the resulting liquid is pure.

only the solid residue is left.

3 Choose the separation method and equipment you would use in each of these situations. Then, describe the stages that would be needed to separate the solutions.

a You want to separate the salt from salt water (so that only the salt remains).

Method: _____

Equipment: _____

Stages: _____

_____

_____

b You want to separate the water from salt water (so that only drinking water remains).

Method: _____

Equipment: _____

Stages: _____

_____

_____

4 Use the words "solid", "liquid", or "gas" to label these diagrams of the distillation process showing how the states of matter change.

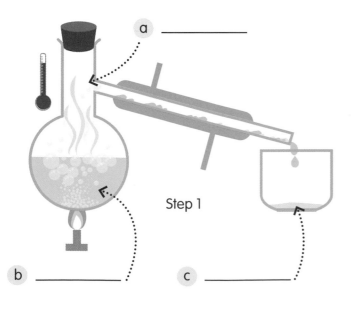

a _____

Step 1

b _____   c _____

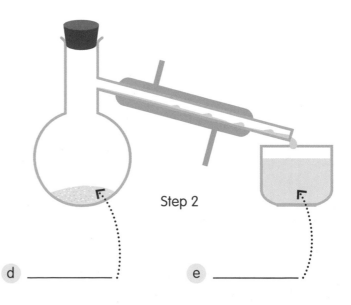

Step 2

d _____   e _____

📖 Pages 128–129

Metals

Typically, metals are hard, shiny, and cold to the touch. There are more than 90 known metals, including iron, gold, and silver. All metals are unique, but they tend to have similar physical properties.

REMEMBER!
Metals are good at conducting heat, but they all conduct heat at different rates.

1 Look at these words carefully and then circle the ones that describe most metals.

| cold | shiny | brittle | solid | hard | malleable | light | reflective | silvery | dull |

2 Use the words "all" or "most" to complete these statements about metals.

a _____ metals are silver in color.

b _____ metals are malleable.

c _____ metals are good at conducting heat.

d _____ metals are good at conducting electricity.

e _____ metals are hard solids.

f _____ metals feel cold.

3 Use the words in the word box to help you complete the three sentences below about the properties of these metals.

| mercury | gold | copper |

a _____ can be scratched.

b _____ is reddish-brown.

c _____ is liquid at room temperature.

4 Draw lines to match these sentence halves about how we use metals.

a (We use metal for cooking equipment because)   (it makes a sound when it is struck.)

b (We use metal for musical instruments because)   (it is a good conductor of heat.)

c (We use metal for electrical devices because)   (it is malleable.)

d (We use metal for making bridges because)   (it is very strong.)

e (We can make metal into thin sheets because)   (it is a good electrical conductor.)

5 Use the words in the word box to help you complete the sentences below.

| aluminum | copper | gold |
| iron | lead | mercury | silver |

a _____ is used in thermometers because it is liquid at room temperature.

b _____ and _____ are used to make jewelry.

c _____ is used to make foil for food.

d _____ is used in electrical wire.

e _____ is used to protect us against radiation.

f _____ is the most commonly used metal.

SCIENCE AT HOME

Conducting heat

Test the heat conductivity of different metal objects at home. You will need tongs, a selection of five small metal objects, some butter, and very warm water from a tap (ask an adult to help you with this).

1. Fill in the names of your objects in the table below.

2. Ask an adult to help you to drop all the objects into the water at the same time.

3. Wait for a few minutes and then use the tongs to carefully take the objects out of the water.

4. Put a small amount of butter on each object at the same time. Which ones melt the butter faster?

Object	Order from 1 to 5, with 1 being the slowest

Pages 156–157

Iron

Iron is the most common and one of the most useful metals on Earth. People have used iron for thousands of years and still use it to make everything from cars to skyscrapers.

REMEMBER!
Iron is quite soft, but when mixed with carbon it forms steel, a very strong metal.

1 Look at these pictures and then number the sentences below to match them.

 1

2

3

 4

a Iron is found in many types of food, including red meat, shellfish, legumes, and green vegetables. ☐

b Iron is found in Earth's core. Earth has a magnetic field due to the iron in its core—iron is a magnetic metal. ☐

c Our bodies use iron to make hemoglobin, a substance found in red blood cells. ☐

d Iron is found in Earth's crust. Iron oxides can make soil and rocks red in color. ☐

2 Underline the correct answers to these questions about iron.

a When did people first discover how to extract iron from soil and rocks?
1000 BCE / 1000 CE / 1,000 years ago

b Which color tells us that iron is present in soil and rocks?
red / blue / green

c How was iron used in the Iron Age?
bridges / tools / ships

d What is added to iron to make it stronger for use in civil engineering?
rock / oxygen / carbon

📖 Page 160

Aluminum

Aluminum is the most common metal in Earth's crust. It is lightweight, easy to shape, and can be mixed with other metals to make strong alloys.

> **DID YOU KNOW?**
> Aluminum can be easily recycled. Recycling uses far less energy than extracting new aluminum.

1 Draw lines to match these uses of aluminum with some of its properties. The first one has been done for you.

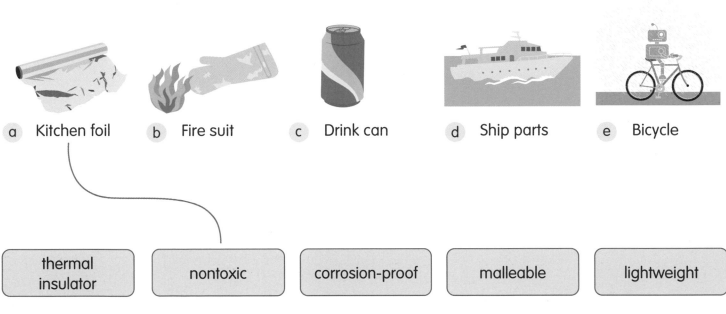

a Kitchen foil   b Fire suit   c Drink can   d Ship parts   e Bicycle

| thermal insulator | nontoxic | corrosion-proof | malleable | lightweight |

2 Number these sentences about the aluminum recycling process to match the correct stages on the diagram.

a The blocks of crushed aluminum are shredded into very small pieces. ☐

b Aluminum objects are collected in recycling bins. ☐

c The small pieces are then rolled into long thin sheets of aluminum. ☐

d The aluminum objects from the recycling bins are crushed into blocks. ☐

e The sheets of aluminum are used to make new products. ☐

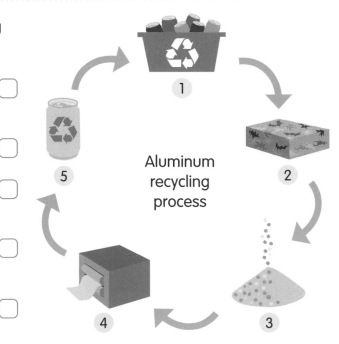

Aluminum recycling process

📖 Page 161

Silver

Pure silver is found in Earth's crust. It is used to make coins and jewelry and also forms light-sensitive compounds that are used in photography and X-rays.

Silver is a precious metal and has been used in coins for thousands of years.

1 Check all the properties below that apply to silver.

a   Liquid at room temperature ☐

b   Good conductor ☐

c   Reddish color ☐

d   Soft ☐

e   Very strong ☐

f   Kills bacteria ☐

g   Light ☐

h   Light-sensitive compounds ☐

2 Identify the properties of silver that make it work well for each of these uses.

Antiseptic: _____

_____

X-rays: _____

_____

Circuit board: _____

_____

Jewelry: _____

_____

3 In parts of the world where there is very little rainfall, silver iodide is sometimes used to make rain. Look at these pictures and number the sentences below to match each one.

1   2   3   4

a   Ice and water droplets cling to the powder and form a cloud. ☐

b   A plane releases silver iodide powder. ☐

c   It begins to rain. ☐

d   The water droplets get heavier. ☐

📖 Page 162

Gold

Gold was one of the first metals to be discovered. Its beauty and rarity make it the most prized metal of all.

The layer of gold inside an astronaut's helmet reflects harmful rays and protects their eyes.

1 Answer these questions about gold.

a Why do gold miners use water or acid?

_____

b Why does gold never lose its shine?

_____

c Why is it safe to eat pure gold?

_____

d Why do we use gold in electronic components?

_____

e How can gold be used to cover picture frames?

_____

2 Read these sentences about gold and then circle true (T) or false (F) for each.

a Gold is usually found in particles in rocks.　　T / F

b Gold can be rolled out so thinly that it becomes transparent.　　T / F

c Gold never loses its shine.　　T / F

d Gold is highly toxic.　　T / F

e Gold is very hard and not ductile.　　T / F

f Gold is expensive.　　T / F

g Gold corrodes over time.　　T / F

h Gold is good at reflecting light rays.　　T / F

📖 Page 163

Carbon

All life on Earth is based on the element carbon. This is because its atoms link together in chains to form millions of different chemicals, called organic compounds.

REMEMBER!
Pure carbon is found in different forms.

1 Look at these pictures of the different forms of pure carbon and then use the words in the word box to help you label each form.

diamond   buckminsterfullerene

amorphous carbon   graphite

a _____

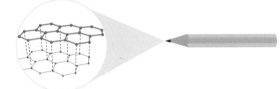

b _____

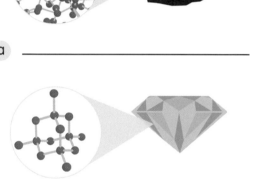

c _____

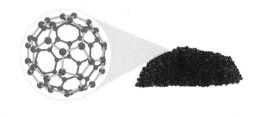

d _____

2 Read these sentences about the different forms of pure carbon and then use the key to help you classify each sentence.

Key   [D] Diamond   [G] Graphite   [A] Amorphous carbon   [B] Buckminsterfullerene

a   It consists of a topsy-turvy jumble of molecules of different shapes.   ☐

b   It forms underground at high temperature and pressure.   ☐

c   It consists of atoms in regular geometric shapes, such as spheres.   ☐

d   The molecules have 60 or more atoms.   ☐

e   It is the hardest natural substance on Earth.   ☐

f   It is very soft.   ☐

g   It is used in pencils and lubricants.   ☐

h   It is found in coal and soot.   ☐

3 Draw lines to match each form of carbon with what it is used for. Then, draw lines to match each completed sentence with the correct picture.

a | Carbon compounds | are very hard and strong and are used as blades in saws that can cut through concrete and even solid rock.

T-shirts and socks

b | Diamonds | from plants are used to make natural fibers, such as cotton.

Propane canister

c | Hydrocarbons | is used to make different types of vehicles because it is very light and very strong.

Diamond blade saw

d | Fine plastic threads | are used in everyday products. For example, propane is used as a fuel in gas grills.

Fleeces and sleeping bags

e | Carbon fiber | are woven together to make synthetic fibers, such as polyester and nylon.

Racing bike

SCIENCE AT HOME

Classify your clothes

What materials are your clothes made from? Look at the labels on a selection of your clothes and complete these lists.

1. Natural fabrics (carbon compounds from animals):

_____

_____

_____

2. Natural fabrics (carbon compounds from plants):

_____

_____

_____

3. Synthetic fabrics (carbon compounds from crude oil):

_____

_____

_____

📖 Pages 166–167

Materials science

Materials science combines the skills of chemists, physicists, and engineers to create new materials with special properties, such as strength, flexibility, or lightness.

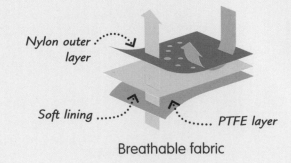

Nylon outer layer

Soft lining ....

.... PTFE layer

Breathable fabric

1 Circle the correct words to complete each of these sentences about composites.

a Composites are made by weaving together or layering **multiple / three** materials.

b Fibers of **flexible / stiff** materials are embedded in the main material.

c This makes the new material very **strong / fragile**.

> **REMEMBER!**
> Some of the most important materials created by scientists and engineers are composites and ceramics.

2 Answer these questions about ceramics.

a What was the first material that ceramic objects were made from?

_____

b What are the properties of that original material—hard or soft, malleable or brittle?

_____

c What did people do to clay to change its properties?

_____

d What happens to the clay when you do this?

_____

e Is the material ancient, or has it been discovered more recently?

_____

f What did people use ceramics for in the past?

_____

g What are some of the new ways in which we use ceramics today?

_____

h Why do you think heat resistance is an important property for car engine parts?

_____

3 Draw lines to match these sentence halves about composites used in the manufacture of cars. Then, number the sentences to match the correct parts of this diagram of a car.

a | Windshields are made with

b | Tires are made with

c | The bodies of some cars are made of

polyester and rubber and layered with steel cords. ☐

threads of carbon woven and set into plastic to make carbon fiber. ☐

two layers of glass and a layer of plastic in between. ☐

4 Use the words in the word box to help you complete the sentences below. Then, number the sentences to match the correct parts of the diagram of a car in question 3.

| bumpers | catalytic converters | piston heads |
| pressure sensors | waterproof trim | car seats |

a _____ absorb toxic fumes from the exhaust. ☐

b EDPM is a synthetic rubber used for _____ around windows. ☐

c Ceramic coatings can help _____ withstand heat. ☐

d _____ are made of polyurethane, so they are light and stiff. ☐

e Ceramic _____ in tires tell the driver when to put more air in. ☐

f _____ are made of a plastic called polypropylene, which is strong and easy to mold. ☐

📖 Pages 176–177

Polymers

Polymers are compounds. Many natural materials,
like wood and wool, are made of polymers.
Some polymers are natural; others, such as
plastics, are artificial.

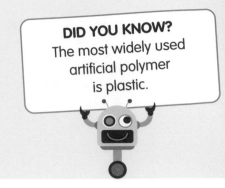

DID YOU KNOW?
The most widely used
artificial polymer
is plastic.

1 Use the words in the word boxes to help you complete the information below about polymers.
Write the artifical polymers in red and the natural polymers in green.

Natural polymers:

| amino acids   casein   cellulose   starch |

Artificial polymers:

| polythene   PVC |

a A fibrous material found in
paper and wood:

_____

b A polymer that melts when it is heated
and hardens when it cools:

_____

c A very hard plastic:

_____

d A polymer found in potatoes and bread:

_____

e A substance found naturally in milk:

_____

f A polymer found in foods high in protein:

_____

2 Answer these questions about natural and artificial polymers.

a How does our body absorb polymers? _____

b What is cellulose made of? _____

c What is the DNA molecule made of? _____

d What is starch made of? _____

e What do we call the two main types of plastics? _____

f What is the main difference between the two? _____

3 Use the words in the word box to help you complete this table about artificial polymers.

> polycarbonate plastic   polystyrene   polythene   PVC

	Properties	Uses
a _____	soft or medium-hard	plastic bags, plastic wrap, and plastic bottles
b _____	very hard	drainpipes and window frames
c _____	easy to mold and light when filled with air	disposable cups
d _____	very hard and transparent	goggles, phones, and sunglasses

4 Plastic is used to make all sorts of everyday items. Use the words from the word box in question 3 to help you identify the type of plastic each of these objects is usually made of.

Sunglasses

Disposable cup

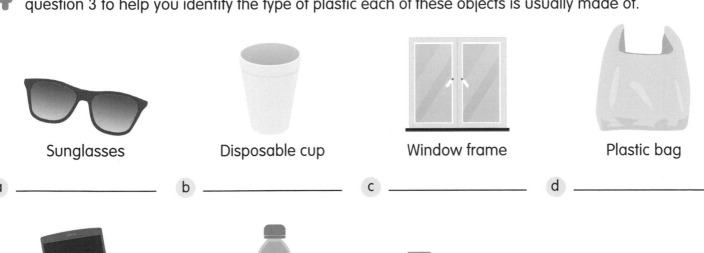
Window frame

Plastic bag

a _____   b _____   c _____   d _____

Cell phone

Plastic bottle

Drainpipe

Takeout food box

e _____   f _____   g _____   h _____

📖 Pages 178–179

What is energy?

Energy is what makes everything happen.
It can be stored or used, but it can't be destroyed.
When you use energy, it doesn't disappear—
it just gets transferred from one form to another.

REMEMBER!
Energy takes many different forms, such as heat, light, sound, and electricity.

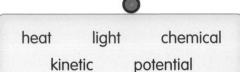

1 Use the words in the word box to help you complete these sentences about the sun's energy. You will need to use some words more than once. Then, number the sentences to match the picture below.

| heat | light | chemical |
| kinetic | potential |

a The sun's energy reaches Earth as _____ and _____ energy. ☐

b Our body stores _____ energy in our muscles. ☐

c The food we eat contains _____ energy stored by plants. ☐

d When you hit the brakes on your bike, the bike's _____ energy is converted to heat and sound energy. ☐

e When you cycle uphill, your muscles transfer _____ energy into _____ energy. ☐

f When you cycle downhill, _____ energy transfers to _____ energy. ☐

2 Draw lines to match each form of energy with the correct application below.

 a Chemical   b Electrical   c Kinetic   d Light    e Potential   f Sound

3 Identify the forms of energy that are being used in the situations below.

a Fire burning in the fireplace:

_____

_____

b The energy in a battery:

_____

_____

c The energy in a flashlight (switched on):

_____

_____

d The energy in a cell phone (switched on):

_____

_____

SCIENCE AT HOME

Energy inventory

Choose a room at home and do an energy inventory.

Name of room: _____

Check the forms of energy you can see and write down the name of the object that is using that energy.

☐ Kinetic _____

☐ Potential _____

☐ Sound _____

☐ Light _____

☐ Heat _____

☐ Chemical _____

☐ Electrical _____

Which is the most common form of energy in the room?

_____

Are any forms of energy not present in the room?

_____

📖 Pages 182–183

Renewable energy

Renewable energy uses sources of energy that never run out or that are replaced by nature faster than we use them.

REMEMBER!
Although renewable energy is kinder to the environment than fossil fuels, it still has an impact on the environment.

1 Draw lines to match each natural resource with the picture that shows the resource being used to generate energy.

| salt water | wind | fresh water | plants | sunlight |

2 Use the words in the word box to help you fill in this table to show how these forms of renewable energy generate electricity.

wind power   hydroelectric power   biomass
tidal and wave power   solar power

a By burning waste plants	b By converting light into electricity	c By turning a turbine

3 Read these sentences about renewable energy power stations and then use the key to help you classify each sentence.

Key

W Wind turbines

S Solar power

T Tidal and wave power

B Biomass

H Hydroelectric power

a The turbines can be placed in the ocean. ☐

b The power stations produce large amounts of electricity. ☐

c Carbon dioxide production can be offset by planting more trees. ☐

d The power stations are placed where there is a lot of sunlight. ☐

e The water from rivers is channeled through turbines. ☐

4 Identify the kind of renewable energy power station we could use to generate electricity in the places shown in these images.

a ____ b ____ c ____ d ____ e ____

____ ____ ____ ____ ____

____ ____ ____ ____ ____

5 Answer these questions about how renewable energy sources are used to generate electricity.

a Which type of renewable energy requires us to change the course of a river? _____

_____

b Biomass-fired power stations produce carbon dioxide, which is not good for the environment.

How is this offset? _____

c Which type of renewable energy doesn't produce energy at night? _____

_____

d Which type of renewable energy is produced offshore? _____

_____

📖 Page 187

Sound

When a sound is made, it causes molecules in the air to vibrate (move back and forth). These vibrations are picked up by your ears as sound.

REMEMBER!
All sounds start as vibrations that spread through the air until they reach your ears.

1 Look at this picture showing how sound waves travel and then number the sentences to show the order in which the process takes place.

a The guitar string vibrates and makes the surrounding air molecules vibrate. ☐

b The air molecules bump into each other. ☐

c Robot 1 plucks the string on his guitar. ☐

d The sound waves reach Robot 2. ☐

e The sound waves spread outward. ☐

f Robot 2 hears the sound. ☐

2 Look at the picture in question 1 and then underline the correct answers to these questions about sound.

a What direction do sound waves move in? **Left to right / Right to left / In all directions**

b What happens to the sound waves? They **come closer together / get farther apart**

c How do they spread? **Toward the source / Away from the source**

d What happens as sound waves get farther from the source? The sound **gets quieter / gets louder**.

e How do all sounds start? As **vibrations / sound waves / air molecules**

f When do we hear a sound? **When the vibrations start / When the sound waves reach us**

3 Answer these questions about how sound travels in space.

a How does all sound start?

_____

b What do vibrations do?

_____

c Which three states of matter can sound travel through?

_____

d Is there any sound at all in outer space? _____

e What is missing in space that is needed for sound to travel? _____

f What do we call a place where there are no air molecules? _____

4 Use the words "solid", "liquid", or "gas" to label each description of the kind of matter sound is travelling through. Then, number the pictures from 1 to 3, with 1 showing where sound is moving the slowest.

a Sound travels through the air

_____

b Sound travels through walls

_____

c Sound travels through water

_____

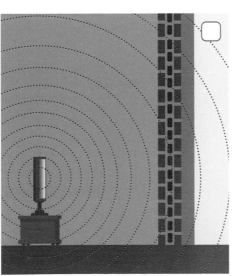

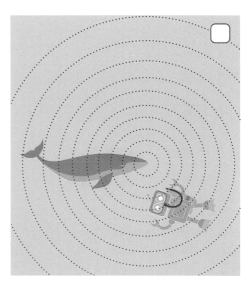

📖 Pages 198–199

Light

Light is a form of energy that we can see. Light travels in waves. It moves so quickly that a beam of light can light up a whole room in an instant.

REMEMBER!
Most solid objects block light. Some materials, like glass and liquid water, let light through.

1 Luminous objects emit, or give off, light. Nonluminous objects reflect light. Draw lines to match each of these objects with the correct description.

 a Sun   b Moon   c Earth   d Candle   e Light bulb

| Emits light | | Reflects light |

 f Mirror    g Fire   h Disco ball   i Window    j Flashlight

2 Read this paragraph about how shadows are formed and then use the underlined words to label the diagram.

A <u>light source</u> illuminates an <u>object</u>. Because light can only move in straight lines, the object blocks the light so a <u>shadow</u> forms behind it. The shadow has two parts. The <u>umbra</u> is the darker part because no light gets through. This is in the center of the shadow. The area around the umbra is called the <u>penumbra</u>. This part is lighter because some of the light gets through.

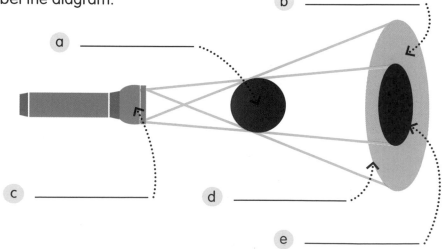

a _____   b _____   c _____   d _____   e _____

3 Use the words in the word box to help you complete the information for each of the pictures below.

transparent	some	translucent	almost all	opaque	no

a   This panel is _____ .

That means _____ light gets through.

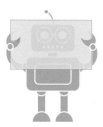

b   This panel is _____ .

That means _____ light gets through.

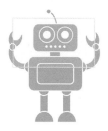

c   This panel is _____ .

That means _____ light gets through.

SCIENCE AT HOME

Light at home

Look at how different objects in your home behave with light. Complete these lists by using examples from your home.

Transparent objects	Translucent objects	Opaque objects

📖 Pages 202–203

Reflection

When light rays bounce off an object, we say they are reflected. Very smooth objects such as mirrors reflect light so well that we can see images in them.

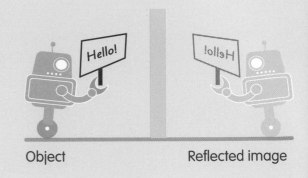

Object   Reflected image

1 Draw arrows onto the diagrams below to show how light rays reflect on different surfaces.

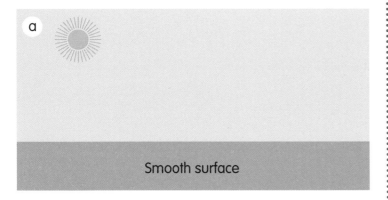

a

Smooth surface

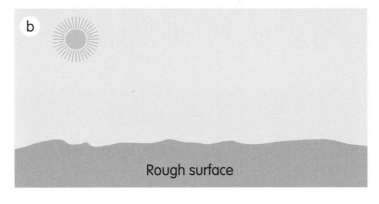

b

Rough surface

2 Hold up an open book in front of a mirror. Use the reflection to help you check the correct answers below.

a Where does the reflected image seem to be?

In the mirror ☐

Behind the mirror ☐

In front of the mirror ☐

b What does the distance seem to be between the image and the mirror?

Much farther than between me and the mirror ☐

Much closer than between me and the mirror ☐

The same distance as between me and the mirror ☐

3 Read these sentences about reflection and then circle true (T) or false (F) for each.

a All objects reflect light.   T / F

b Rough surfaces scatter the light rays.   T / F

c Rough surfaces don't reflect any light.   T / F

d Mirrors reverse things from left to right.   T / F

e Mirrors reverse things from front to back.   T / F

f Mirrors contain a sheet of plastic that reflects light.   T / F

4 Check the objects that reflect enough light for us to see our reflection in.

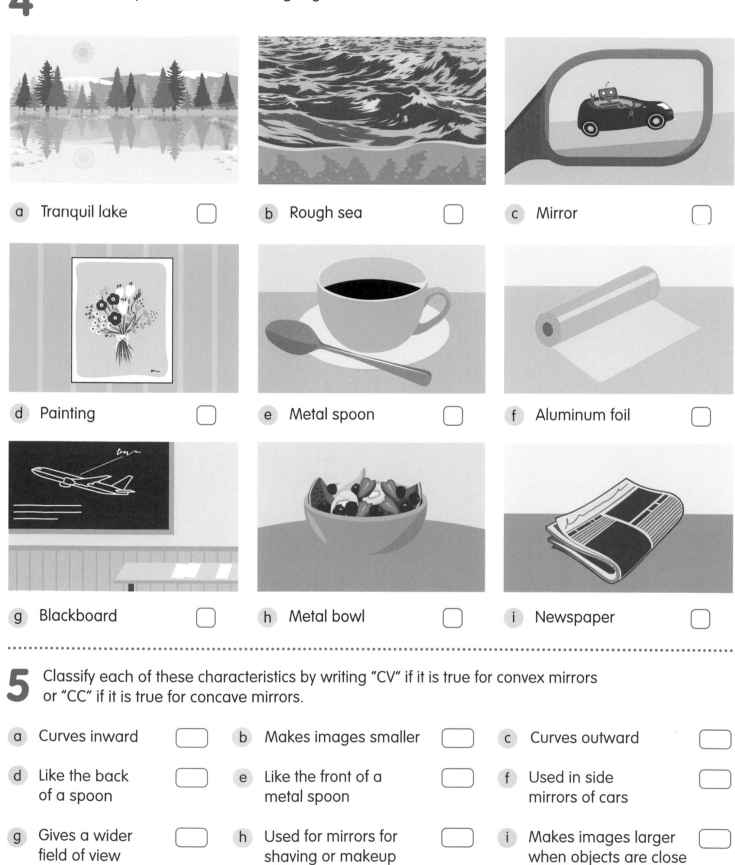

a Tranquil lake ☐

b Rough sea ☐

c Mirror ☐

d Painting ☐

e Metal spoon ☐

f Aluminum foil ☐

g Blackboard ☐

h Metal bowl ☐

i Newspaper ☐

5 Classify each of these characteristics by writing "CV" if it is true for convex mirrors or "CC" if it is true for concave mirrors.

a Curves inward ☐

b Makes images smaller ☐

c Curves outward ☐

d Like the back of a spoon ☐

e Like the front of a metal spoon ☐

f Used in side mirrors of cars ☐

g Gives a wider field of view ☐

h Used for mirrors for shaving or makeup ☐

i Makes images larger when objects are close ☐

📖 Pages 204–205

Forming images

An image is a copy of an object, but it may be smaller or larger than the object or inverted (upside down). Lenses can be used to create images of objects.

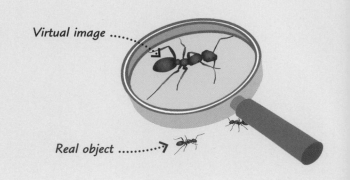

Virtual image ....

Real object ....➔

1 Use the words in the word box to help you complete these sentences about images.

| lens | magnifying | pinhole |
| projector | real | virtual |

a   An image you see when you look through a lens is called a _____ image.

b   An image you see on a screen is called a _____ image.

c   When you look at an image through a _____ glass, it looks larger.

d   You can display an image on a screen by using a _____ .

e   You can create a real image without a lens by using a _____ camera.

f   Cameras and eyes use a _____ to create a real image.

....

2 Several devices can be used to produce real images. Use "projector" (P), "pinhole camera" (PC), or "camera" (C) to first label these pictures and then classify the sentences below.

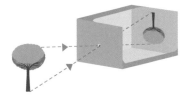 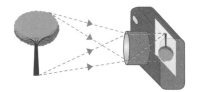

a   _____   b   _____   c   _____

d   The image passes through a large hole.   ☐   e   The image passes through a small hole.   ☐

f   The image is displayed on a screen.   ☐   g   The image is held in a tape.   ☐

h   The image is sharp and very bright.   ☐   i   The image is sharp but very faint.   ☐

Telescopes and microscopes

Telescopes and microscopes use lenses or mirrors to create magnified images. Telescopes create magnified images of distant objects. Microscopes create magnified images of nearby but tiny objects.

1 Use the words in the word box to help you label the microscope and the telescope below. You will need to use some words for both diagrams.

focusing knob	focusing dial	eyepiece
objective lens	lamp or mirror	object to be studied

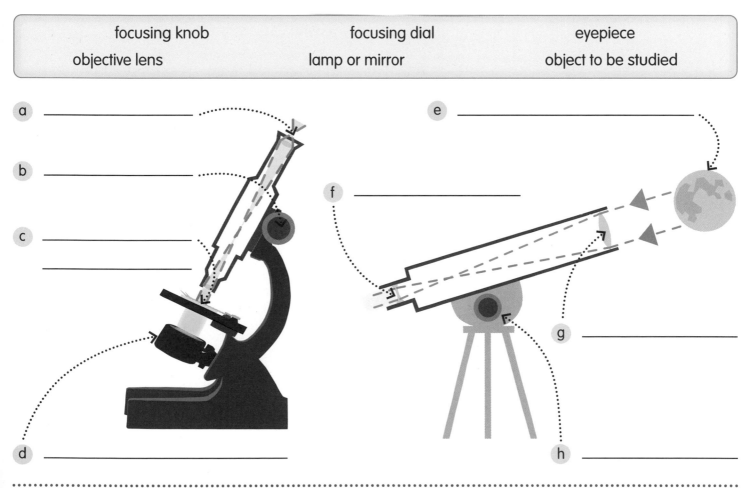

a _____

b _____

c _____

_____

d _____

e _____

f _____

g _____

h _____

2 Draw lines to match each thing listed below with the device that you would use to observe it.

a Molecules

b Comets

c Jupiter

Microscope

Telescope

d Cells in an insect's body

e Bacteria

f Wildlife that is far away

Pages 210–211

Colors

The world is full of colors, from the bright blue of the sky to the deep red of a tomato. All these colors are simply the way our eyes see different wavelengths of light.

REMEMBER!
White light is a mixture of all the colors. Each color travels on a different wavelength.

1 Number these sentences to match the correct stages on the diagram below to show what happens when light is shone through a prism.

a The prism bends the beam of light. ☐

b The colors fan out to form a spectrum. ☐

c White light is shone into a prism. ☐

d Every color has a different wavelength, and the prism bends each wavelength in a different way. ☐

2 Look at this picture of a leaf and then answer the questions below.

a What color does the leaf reflect? _____

b What colors does the leaf absorb? _____

c What is the result of this? _____

3 Look carefully at this diagram of a rainbow and circle the robot that can see it. Then, read the sentences below and circle true (T) or false (F) for each.

a There is no rainbow if there are no water droplets.　T / F

b There are rainbows when it is dark at night.　T / F

c The water droplets make all the colors look white.　T / F

d There are seven colors in the spectrum.　T / F

e The colors in a rainbow are in the same order as the colors in a spectrum from a prism.　T / F

4 Answer these questions about colors and light.

a What are the three primary colors of light?

_____

b How are they different from the three primary colors of paint?

_____

c What happens if we mix two of the primary colors of light?

_____

d Do we get the same color if we mix any two primary colors of light?

_____

e What happens when we mix all three primary colors of light?

_____

REMEMBER!
All the millions of colors that we can see are made by mixing just three different colors of light.

SCIENCE AT HOME

Separating light

You will need a full glass of water, two pieces of white paper, a flashlight, a pair of scissors, and sticky tape.

1. Cut a small slit in one of the pieces of paper and tape it to the side of the glass in such a way that light can pass through the slit onto the surface of the water.

2. Put the other piece of paper on the floor in front of the glass, turn off the lights, and switch on the flashlight.

3. Shine the beam through the slit, making sure it hits the water's surface and the paper on the floor. Gently move the flashlight and the glass around until you can see the spectrum of colors on the paper on the floor.

📖 Pages 212–213

Electromagnetic spectrum

Light energy is a form of radiation that travels in waves that we can see. Radiation also travels in waves, but these are too short or too long for our eyes to see. Together with light, all these different wavelengths make up the electromagnetic spectrum.

1 Circle the correct words or phrases to complete each of these sentences about the electromagnetic spectrum.

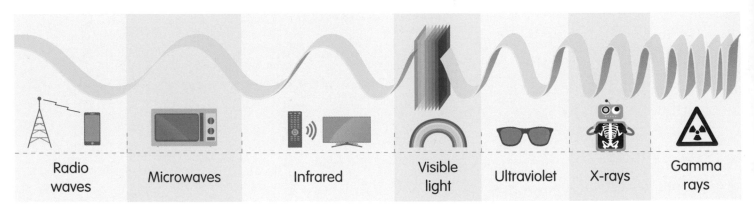

| Radio waves | Microwaves | Infrared | Visible light | Ultraviolet | X-rays | Gamma rays |

a Electromagnetic waves are **all the same length / many different lengths**.

b Visible light makes up **a small part of / all of** the electromagnetic spectrum.

c The longest waves are **radio waves / gamma rays**.

d X-rays are **shorter / longer** electromagnetic waves than infrared waves.

e Electromagnetic waves that come after visible light are **longer / shorter** than electromagnetic waves that come before visible light.

f Microwaves are **shorter / longer** electromagnetic waves than ultraviolet waves.

2 Use the words in the word box to help you identify the electromagnetic waves involved in each of these situations below.

| gamma rays | X-rays |
| ultraviolet | radio waves |

a Used to make images of skeletons:

_____

b Can be seen by many birds and insects:

_____

c Give off radioactive substances that kill living cells: _____

d Used to transmit phone calls and Internet data:

_____

Static electricity

If you rub a balloon on a sweater and then hold it against a wall, it will stay there. It's held in place by the same thing that causes lightning: static electricity.

REMEMBER!
Objects have positive and negative charges. Objects with opposite charges attract each other. Objects with the same charge repel each other

1 Use the key to help you draw arrows between these pairs of balloons to show if they will repel or attract each other. Then, circle the pairs that show static electricity.

Key →←— Attract   ←——→ Repel

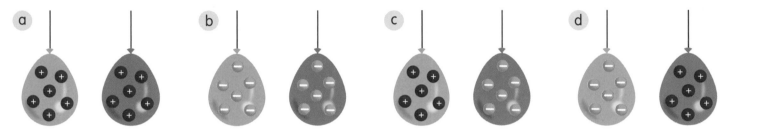

a   b   c   d

....

2 Look at these pictures and then check the ones that show static electricity.

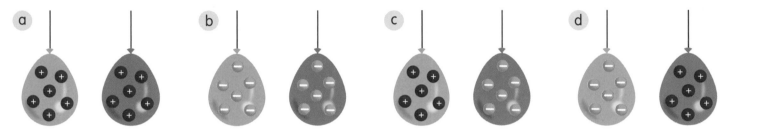

a Light bulb lighting up ☐   b Bolt of lightning ☐   c Electric shock from a car door ☐

d Television switching on ☐   e Balloon sticking to a wall ☐   f Comb lifting your hair ☐

📖 Pages 218–219

Current electricity

Unlike static electricity, which stays in one place, current electricity moves. All the electrical devices that we use rely on flowing electric current.

REMEMBER!
Materials that allow electricity to flow are called conductors.
Materials that don't allow electricity to flow are called insulators.

1 Materials that allow electricity to flow through them are called conductors, while materials that block electricity are called insulators. Draw lines to match each of these objects with the correct description.

   **a**   Lemon juice

   **b**   Tap water

   **c**   Copper

   **d**   Rubber

   **e**   Cork

Conductor		Insulator

   **f**   Gold

   g   Silver

   **h**   Wood

   i   Wool

   j   Paper

2 Read these sentences about conductors and then circle true (T) or false (F) for each.

a   Many metals are good conductors.   T / F   **b**   Tap water isn't a good conductor.   T / F

c   Gold and silver are used for electrical wiring in houses.   T / F   **d**   It's dangerous to touch electrical objects with wet hands.   T / F

e   Insulators allow the flow of electricity.   T / F   **f**   Plastic can pick up static electricity.   T / F

g   Electrical wires are coated in plastic or rubber.   T / F   **h**   Copper is a good insulator.   T / F

3

Answer these questions about conductors and insulators.

a) Which metal is usually used as an electrical conductor in wires and cables?

_____

b) Gold is a good conductor, but it isn't used in large devices. Why not?

_____

c) Why should you never touch electrical objects with wet hands?

_____

d) Why do you get a small electric shock if you walk on a plastic carpet with plastic shoes?

_____

e) Which materials are good for coating electric wires and plugs?

_____

f) Which type of liquids are known to be good electrical conductors?

_____

4

Use the words in the word box to help you label this diagram of a battery.

| anode   cathode   electrolyte   positive charge   negative charge   battery   light bulb |

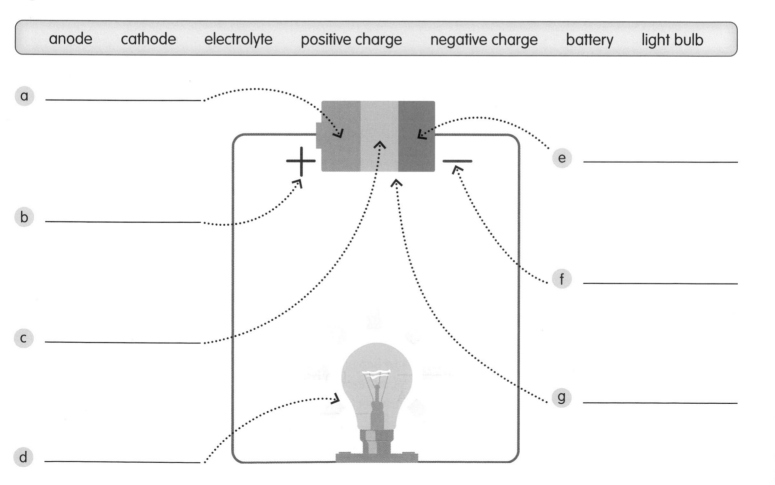

a _____

b _____

c _____

d _____

e _____

f _____

g _____

Electric circuits

All the electrical devices that we use, from phones to TVs, depend on electricity flowing through circuits. When a circuit is switched on, it forms a complete loop without any gaps.

REMEMBER!
Small devices in an electric circuit are called components.

1 Look at the words in the word box and circle the components that are used in these electric circuits. Then, color in the bulbs that have an electric current flowing through them.

| battery | bulb | computer | buzzer | circuit breaker | plug | fuse | switch | wire |

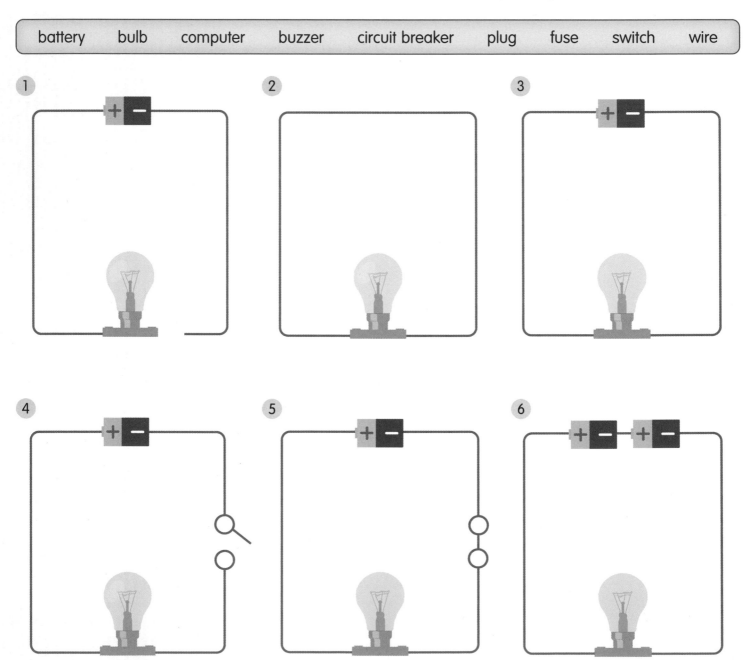

2 Look at the circuits in question 1 and then number these sentences to match the correct circuits.

a The light bulb is working and is even brighter because there is more energy. ☐

b The light bulb isn't working because the switch isn't on. ☐

c The light bulb is working because the circuit is complete and the switch is on. ☐

d The light bulb isn't working because there is a gap in the circuit. ☐

e The light bulb is working because the circuit is complete. ☐

f The light bulb isn't working because there is no battery. ☐

3 Check the correct answers to these questions about circuits.

a What do electrical devices need in order to work?

A completed circuit with a flowing electrical current. ☐

A battery and a switch. ☐

b What happens when you add another battery to an electrical circuit?

The light bulb explodes. ☐

There is more voltage for the bulb, so the light will be brighter. ☐

c What happens when you add another bulb to an electrical circuit?

There is less voltage for each bulb, so the lights will be dimmer. ☐

The light bulb turns off. ☐

d What happens when a switch in an electrical circuit is open?

The electrical current flows. ☐

The electrical current doesn't flow. ☐

SCIENCE AT HOME

Make an electrical circuit

You will need a battery, two lengths of copper wire, a small light bulb, and some sticky tape to hold the wires in place.

Attach one wire to the negative end of the battery and wrap its other end around the metal base of the bulb. Attach the other wire to the positive end of the battery and to the bulb's metal base. This will complete the circuit and light up the bulb.

Battery

Copper wire

Light bulb

Metal base of the light bulb

📖 Pages 222–223

What are forces?

A force makes an object move. When we kick a ball or ride a bike, we use forces. Forces can make things start or stop moving, go faster or slower, change direction, or even change shape.

When the man pulls the suitcase, the force in his arm makes the suitcase move forward.

1 Use the words "pulled" or "pushed" to complete these sentences about force. Then, draw arrowheads on the blue lines to show the direction of movement.

a   The football is being

_____

by the player's foot.

b   The bowstring is being

_____

by the archer.

c   The pedals are being

_____

by the cyclist's feet.

d   The skateboard is being

_____

by gravity.

e   The weights are being

_____

up by the weightlifter.

SCIENCE AT HOME

Push or pull?

Think about everyday things that you might do at home and what kind of force you exert in each activity. Is it a push or a pull? Could you be doing both?

Opening a window

_____

Closing a door

_____

Using a vacuum cleaner

_____

Opening and closing a drawer

_____

Opening a book

_____

Drying the dishes

_____

Getting dressed

_____

2 Look at this picture and then use the words in the word box to help you complete the sentences below. You will need to use some words twice.

| bowstring | gravity | bend | leg | move | target | fall | upward | archer's arm | stop |

a The archer pulls the bowstring.

The force in the _____ makes the bow _____ .

b The archer releases the bowstring.

The force in the _____ makes the arrow _____ .

c The arrow hits the target.

The force in the _____ makes the arrow _____ .

d The soccer player kicks the ball.

The force in the soccer player's _____ makes the ball move _____ .

e The ball moves through the air.

The force of _____ makes the ball _____ .

Pages 234–235

Stretching and deforming

When forces act on an object that can't move, the object may change shape or even break. These changes are called deformations.

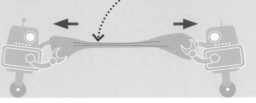

If an object's shape changes permanently, like a piece of stretched chewing gum, the object is said to be plastic.

1 In this word snake, circle six words that describe how different materials react when force is exerted on them. Use the words in the word box to help you.

| deform | shatter | smash | stretch | break | snap |

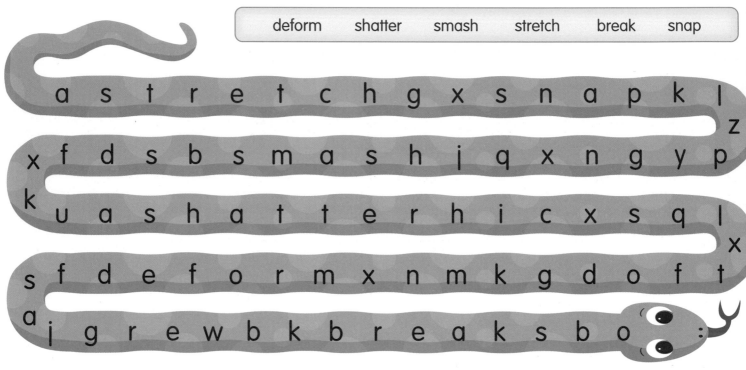

a s t r e t c h g x s n a p k l
z
x f d s b s m a s h j q x n g y p
k
u a s h a t t e r h i c x s q l
x
s f d e f o r m x n m k g d o f t
a
j g r e w b k b r e a k s b o

2 Use the words in the word box to help you complete these definitions.

| brittle | plastic | elastic |

a _____ materials stretch when force is applied to them. When the force is removed, they return to their original shape.

Rubber band

b _____ materials stretch when force is applied to them, but they don't go back to their original shape when the force is removed.

Plastic wrap

c _____ materials snap, shatter, or smash when force is applied to them.

China cup

3 Draw arrows on each shape to show the direction of the force applied. Use the original shapes as reference. Then, use the words in the word box to help you label the forces.

| compression | tension |
| bending | twisting |

a _____

b _____

c _____

d _____

When forces push an object from opposite directions, it is squeezed and may bulge.

When forces pull an object from opposite directions, it gets stretched.

When forces act in different places and in opposite directions, the object will twist.

When forces act in different places and in different directions, the object will bend.

4 Draw lines to match these sentence halves about stretching and deforming.

a Stretching or deforming

b All objects break

c Brittle objects

d Some objects change shape

e Forces act in different directions

f The way objects deform

g Some forces called torques

h Objects won't return to their original shape

and this produces different changes in shape.

and we say they deform.

depends on the number and directions of the forces.

happens when forces act on an object that can't move.

if enough force is applied to them.

if you stretch them past their elastic limit.

shatter or snap when forces act on them.

twist objects.

📖 Pages 236–237

Magnetism

Magnetism is a force that can push or pull objects without touching them. Magnets only pull objects made of certain materials.

REMEMBER
Every magnet is surrounded by a magnetic field—a zone in which objects are pulled.

1 Use the words in the word box to help you complete these sentences about magnets and magnetism.

attract	north	pull
push	south	whole

a   Magnets _____ objects made of certain materials,

such as iron, nickel, and steel.

b   A magnet has two ends: a _____ pole and a _____ pole.

c   Magnets _____ apart when the same poles are close.

d   Magnets _____ together when opposite poles are close.

e   If you cut a bar magnet in half, each half immediately becomes a

_____ magnet with two poles.

....

2 Circle the correct words to complete each of these sentences about the magnets in the pictures. Then tick the correct explanation of how magnetism works.

a   The magnets **attract / repel** each other.

b   The magnets **attract / repel** each other.

c   The magnets **attract / repel** each other.

d   Two magnets pull each other if opposite poles come close. ☐

Two magnets pull each other if the same poles come close. ☐

Two magnets pull each other if any poles come close. ☐

3 Underline the correct answers to these questions about magnetism.

a) What are all magnets surrounded by?
A magnetic field / Iron filings

b) What shape are the lines in a magnetic field?
Straight / Curved

c) How many poles do magnets have?
One pole / Two poles

d) Where is the magnetic field strongest?
Close to the magnet / Far from the magnet

e) Where is the "magnet" in Earth?
In the center of Earth / At the North Pole

f) Where does the needle on a compass point?
North / South

· ·

4 Circle the names of the objects that would be pulled toward a magnet. Then, answer the question below.

a) Cork

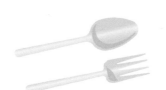

b) Steel cutlery

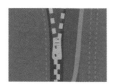

c) Zip

d) Cast iron pot

e) China cup

f) Glass

g) What do all the objects you have circled have in common?

They are all made of metal. ☐

They are all kitchen objects. ☐

SCIENCE AT HOME

Make your own compass

Follow these steps to make a compass and then answer the question below.

You will need a plate of water, a needle, a magnet, a cork, and some sticky tape.

1. Magnetize the needle by rubbing it several times along the magnet. Always rub it in the same direction. Once you have magnetized one side of the needle, repeat the procedure on the other side.

2. Attach the needle to the cork with sticky tape.

3. Float the cork on the water. Make a note of which direction the needle is pointing in.

Ask an adult to help you use your compass to identify the direction your house faces.

My house faces _____ .

📖 Pages 240–241

Friction

When an object slides across another object, a force called friction slows it down. The rougher the surfaces, the greater the friction. Friction is the enemy of motion, but sometimes it's a good thing, as it gives you grip.

DID YOU KNOW?
We need friction to be able to move around.

1 Circle the correct words or phrases to complete each of these sentences about friction.

a Friction is a force that **slows things down / speeds things up**.

b Friction happens when two solid objects **rub against / repel** each other.

c Friction always generates an energy transfer of **heat / light**.

d Friction **wears away / builds up** parts in a machine that rub together.

e Without friction, we would **slip on / grip** the floor as we walk.

f The pattern of the tread on tires **increases / decreases** friction.

2 Look at these pictures and then check the one in each pair that shows the least friction.

a

Walking in socks

Walking in shoes

b

Driving on a road

Skating on ice

c

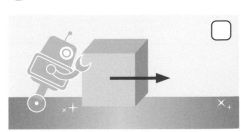

Pushing a box on a shiny surface

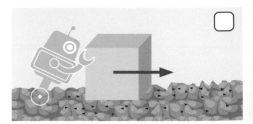

Pushing a box on a rough surface

3 Answer these questions about friction.

a How does friction help us walk?

_____

b Why do many vehicles have wheels?

_____

c What part of a car uses friction to slow down?

_____

d What happens in machinery where there is friction over long periods of time?

_____

e What can we use to reduce friction in machinery?

_____

f Which carpenters' tools deliberately increase friction?

_____

4 Draw lines to match each picture with the correct sentence about friction.

a

There is friction between the surface of the road and the wheels. This stops us from slipping all over the road.

b

There is friction in the handlebars so that our hands can grip them.

c

The brakes exert friction on the wheels of the bike so that we can stop.

d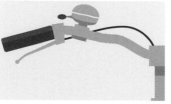

There is friction between the pedals and our shoes so that our feet don't slip off the pedals.

Pages 242–243

Drag

When objects move through air or water, they have to overcome a force called drag. Smooth surfaces and streamlined shapes help reduce this force.

REMEMBER!
Sometimes we deliberately use drag in order to slow things down.

1 Look at these pictures of a javelin and a cardboard box moving through the air. Draw lines around the objects to show the effects of drag. Then, answer the questions below.

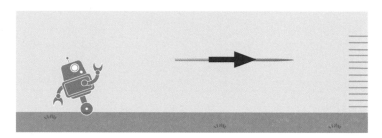 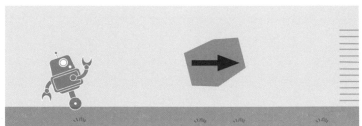

a   Why does drag happen? _____

_____

b   What does drag do to moving objects? _____

c   Why do small objects have less drag than large objects? _____

_____

2 Read these sentences about drag and turbulence and then circle true (T) or false (F) for each.

a   Drag is caused by friction with the road.   T / F

b   Drag is like friction, but caused by air or water.   T / F

c   The slower an object moves, the more turbulence it causes.   T / F

d   Turbulent air takes kinetic energy from a moving vehicle.   T / F

e   Animals such as sharks and dolphins are streamlined.   T / F

f   The more streamlined an object is, the more drag it causes.   T / F

3 Circle the two streamlined objects or animals in each category below.

a Vehicles:

Tractor

Sports car

Aeroplane

Bus

b Animals:

Panda

Bird

Dolphin

Elephant

c Sports equipment:

Target

Bicycle

Canoe

Soccer goal

4 Number the sentences below to match the correct stages in this diagram of a skydiver.

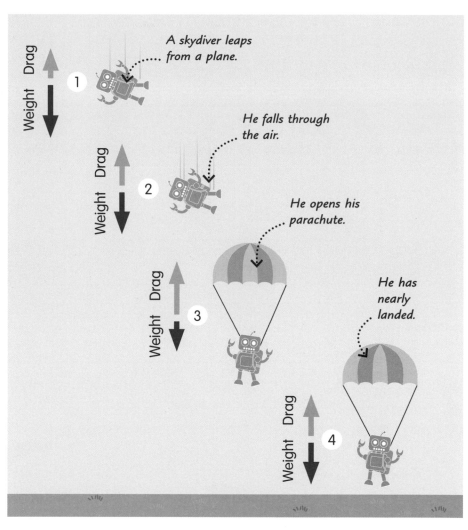

Drag · Weight

A skydiver leaps from a plane. 1

He falls through the air. 2

He opens his parachute. 3

He has nearly landed. 4

a The skydiver's body reaches a steady, but much slower, speed because the force of his weight is the same as the force of drag. ☐

b The skydiver's body accelerates because the force of his weight is greater than the force of drag. ☐

c The skydiver's body decelerates because the force of his weight is much less than the force of drag. ☐

d The skydiver's body moves at a steady speed because the force of his weight is the same as the force of drag. ☐

📖 Pages 244–245

Simple machines

Simple machines work by changing how much force you need to do something. Most of them work by increasing a force, making a tough job much easier.

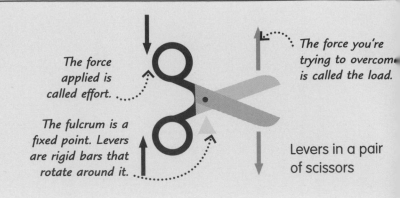

The force applied is called effort.

The fulcrum is a fixed point. Levers are rigid bars that rotate around it.

The force you're trying to overcome is called the load.

Levers in a pair of scissors

---

1 Check the correct answers to these questions about simple machines.

a Why do we use machines to do work?

Because we don't need to apply as much force, making a job easier ☐

Because they make our work more precise ☐

b What is the mechanical advantage of a machine?

The amount by which the machine multiplies the force needed for a job ☐

The amount of energy a machine uses to do a job ☐

....

2 These tools are all forms of levers. Circle the fulcrum and then draw arrows to show the direction of effort and load for each one.

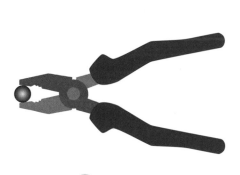

a Pliers

b Wheelbarrow

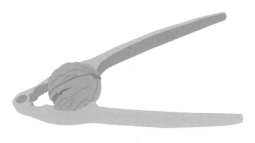

c Nutcracker

d Tongs

3 Use the words in the word box to help you complete the information for each ramp below.

| less | long | more | short | shallow | steep |

REMEMBER!
Both levers and ramps are simple machines.

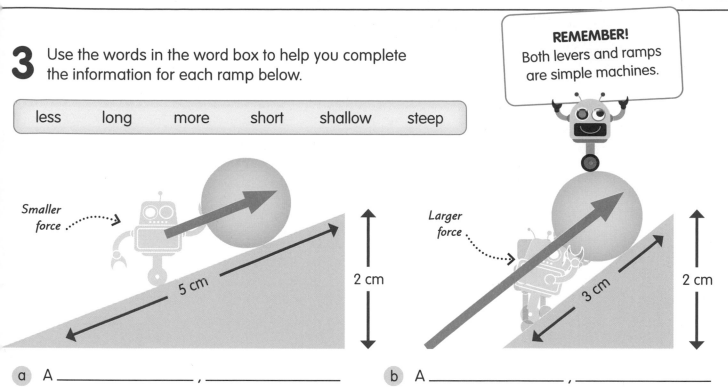

Smaller force

5 cm

2 cm

Larger force

3 cm

2 cm

a A _____ , _____ slope requires _____ force.

b A _____ , _____ slope requires _____ force.

4 Use this formula with the measurements from question 3 to calculate the mechanical advantage of each ramp above.

distance ÷ height = mechanical advantage

a Mechanical advantage formula:

_____ ÷ _____ = _____

b Mechanical advantage formula:

_____ ÷ _____ = _____

SCIENCE AT HOME

Make a catapult

A catapult is a type of lever. Follow the instructions below to make your own working catapult.

You will need:
ten craft sticks (or ice cream sticks), five rubber bands, a plastic spoon, and a load, such as a ball of paper.

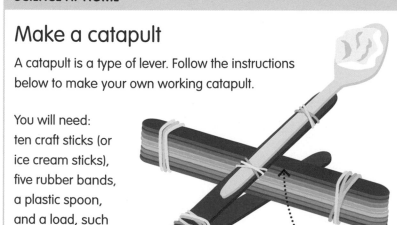

Fulcrum

1. Wind rubber bands around both ends of a pile of eight craft sticks. A point on the pile of sticks will act as the fulcrum.

2. Place one craft stick underneath and another on top of the pile of craft sticks. Secure these two craft sticks at one end with another rubber band.

The top craft stick is the bar of the lever.

3. Secure the plastic spoon to the bar with rubber bands, as shown in the picture.

4. Put your load in the spoon, pull down on it, and let go to see how well your catapult works.

📖 Pages 250–251

More simple machines

Levers and ramps aren't the only simple machines. Pulleys, screws, and wheels can also magnify forces and make jobs easier to do.

> **REMEMBER!**
> Most tools include more than one simple machine. Scissors, for example, have a wedge and a lever.

1 Use the words in the word box to help you label these pictures of simple machines.

| pulley | screw | wedge | wheel and axle |

a _____

b _____

c _____

d _____

2 Use the words from the word box in question 1 to help you complete this table about simple machines.

	a _____	b _____	c _____	d _____
Name of machine				
Description	Thick at one end and thin at the other	Spiral	Circular discs with central rod	Rope and wheel
Direction of force	Downward and sideways	Circular	Circular	Downward
Uses	Splitting objects	Driving objects into hard surfaces	Transporting objects and people	Lifting weights

3 Draw lines to match each task with the simple machine
that would be the most useful for that job.

To wheel a wheelchair into an entrance	To place under a door to stop it from closing	To lift a pile of bricks to the roof of a house

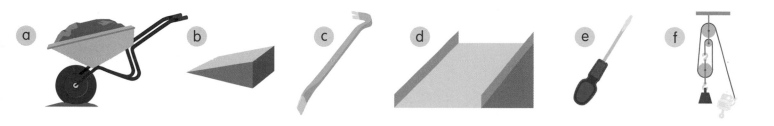

a b c d e f

To move bags of soil in the garden	To fix a shelf to the wall	To take the top off a can of paint

....

4 Identify two simple machines that are part of these complex tools.
Write their names under each tool.

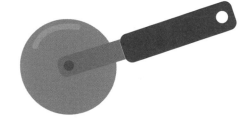

a _____ , _____

b _____ , _____

c _____ , _____

d _____ , _____

📖 Pages 252–253

Gravity

Whenever you drop something, it falls because it's pulled down by a force called gravity. Gravity works throughout the universe. It holds planets, stars, and galaxies together.

REMEMBER!
All bits of matter, big and small, pull on each other with the force of gravity.

1 Imagine a robot in three different situations: on Earth, on the moon, and in outer space. Look at these pictures and then answer the questions below.

Weight: 245 N   Weight: 40 N   Weight: 0 N

a Why does the robot weigh more on Earth than on the moon?

_____

b Is the mass of the robot the same on the Moon and in outer space as on Earth?

_____

c Does the robot weigh the same on Earth as in outer space?

_____

d How much does the robot weigh in outer space?

_____

2 Check the correct answers to these questions about gravity.

a What is gravity?

It is a force ☐
It is a molecule ☐

b Where does gravity work?

Over the land on Earth ☐
Everywhere in the universe ☐

c Is gravity stronger in objects with more mass?

Yes, it is ☐
No, it makes no difference ☐

3 Use the words in the word box to help you complete these sentences.

force

mass

accelerate

more

pull

weight

a An object's _____ is how much matter there is in it.

b An object's _____ tells us how strongly gravity pulls on it.

c Gravity makes objects _____ .

d Objects that are very far apart have a weak gravitational _____ .

e Objects with _____ mass have more gravity.

f Weight is a _____ , but mass isn't.

4 Read these sentences about gravity and then circle true (T) or false (F) for each.

a Gravity works by making objects accelerate.　　T / F

b Falling objects accelerate as they fall.　　T / F

c Gravity is a very strong force.　　T / F

d Light objects always fall faster than heavy objects.　　T / F

e If there was no air, all objects would accelerate at exactly the same rate.　　T / F

REMEMBER!
If there was no air to get in the way, all objects, whatever they weigh, would accelerate to Earth at exactly the same rate, falling 10 meters per second (m/s) faster with each passing second.

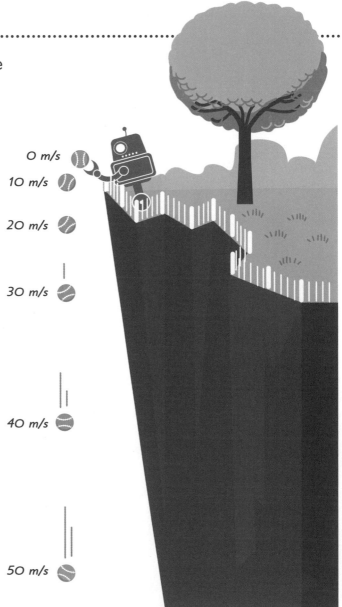

0 m/s

10 m/s

20 m/s

30 m/s

40 m/s

50 m/s

Pages 258–259

Flight

Planes are heavier than air, yet they can take off
from the ground and fly above the clouds. They use
fast-flowing air to generate a force known as lift.

REMEMBER!
The wings of a plane
create the force of lift, which
counters the force of gravity.

1 Answer these questions about how planes fly.

a) Which force do planes need to create to fly? _____

b) Which force is opposite of lift? _____

c) What must a plane do in order to create lift? _____

d) What happens to the air around the plane when it accelerates? _____
_____

e) As the plane moves forward, what happens to most of the air? _____
_____

f) Which part of the wing is higher, the front or the back? _____

2 Circle the correct words to complete each of these sentences about how wings
are used in flight. Then, number the sentences to match the pictures.

a) The air pressure under the wings is **higher** / **lower** than above the wings. ☐

b) The wings have a special shape called an airfoil, which means the ☐
top is **more** / **less** curved than the bottom.

c) The wings on a plane are **higher** / **lower** at the front than at the back. ☐

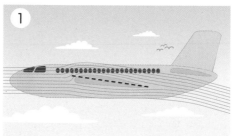

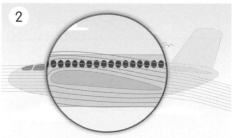

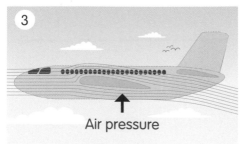

Air pressure

3 Pilots use several devices to control the movement of a plane. Draw lines to match each picture with the correct description.

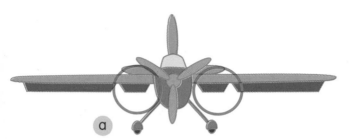

a

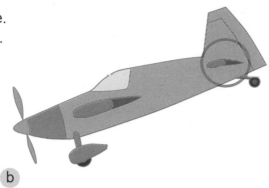

b

Ailerons are long flaps on the wings. They make the plane roll, which helps it turn.

The rudder is a flap on the tail. It makes the plane turn left or right.

The elevators are flaps at the back of the plane. They lift or drop the nose of the plane.

The short flaps on the wings are like brakes, and they increase the force of drag.

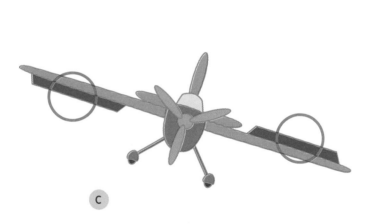

c

d

SCIENCE AT HOME

Paper planes

Make some paper planes and see how long they stay in the air and how far they travel.

1. Fold three pieces of paper to make three types of plane. Try a basic dart, a tricky zip dart, and an intermediate V-wing.

2. Mark a starting line on the ground and throw each plane at least three times. Time how long each plane stayed in the air and then measure the total distance it traveled. Which plane went the farthest? Which stayed aloft the longest? Why do you think that was? What made it different from the other planes?

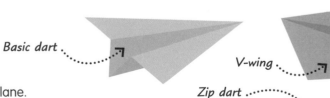

Basic dart

V-wing

Zip dart

📖 Pages 260–261

Floating and sinking

Some things float on water, such as boats. Others sink, such as stones. This is because things that float are lighter than water, and things that sink are heavier.

> **REMEMBER!**
> The weight of an object in water pushes the water out of the way. This creates a force called upthrust.

1 Look at this picture, then number the sentences below to match the objects in the picture.

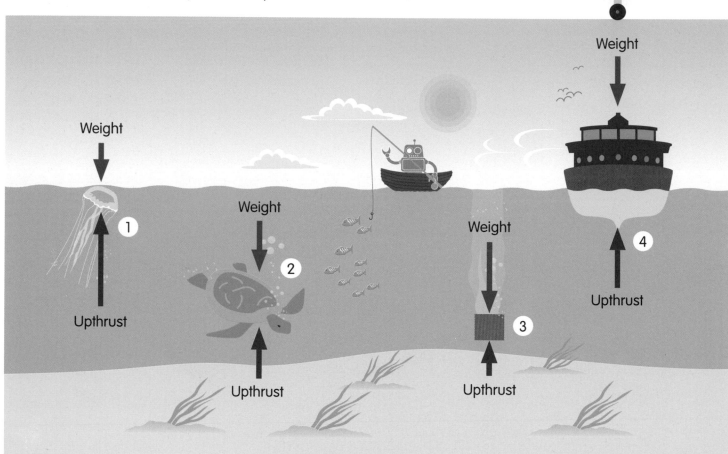

a If an object weighs the same as an equal volume of water, the upthrust equals the object's weight. The object has neutral buoyancy. ☐

b If an object weighs less than an equal volume of water, the upthrust is greater than the object's weight. The object rises to the surface. ☐

c If an object weighs more than an equal volume of water, the upthrust is less than the object's weight. The object sinks. ☐

d If a solid, heavy object contains a lot of air, it will float. ☐

2 Circle the correct words to complete each of these sentences about floating and sinking.

a A solid block of steel will **sink / float** because its weight is **greater / less** than the force of the upthrust.

b A steel ship will **sink / float** because it is full of **air / water**, so its weight is **greater / less** than the force of the upthrust.

c A submarine can float by filling its tanks with **air / water**, or it can sink by filling its tanks with **air / water**.

d All objects weigh **less / more** when they are underwater.

3 Calculate the amount of water displaced by each of these weights.

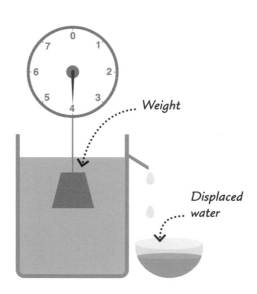
Weight
Displaced water

a Weight in water   = 45 kg   Water displacement

Weight out of water = 90 kg   = _____

b Weight in water   = 25 kg   Water displacement

Weight out of water = 42 kg   = _____

c Weight in water   = 12 kg   Water displacement

Weight out of water = 18 kg   = _____

4 Draw lines to match these sentence halves about how submarines float and dive.

a A submarine is surrounded by   can hold air or water.

b The ballast tanks   control the air.

c When the ballast tanks are full of air, large spaces called ballast tanks.

d When the ballast tanks are full of water, the submarine floats.

e Vents at the top   when the ballast tanks are full of water.

f The submarine is denser than the water   the submarine sinks.

📖 Pages 264–265

The Universe

The universe is everything that exists. It includes planets, stars, galaxies, and vast expanses of space that stretch farther than we can see.

DID YOU KNOW?
Nobody really knows how big the universe is. It might be infinite.

1 Use the words in the word box to help you label this picture.

| galaxy | solar system |
| planet | universe |

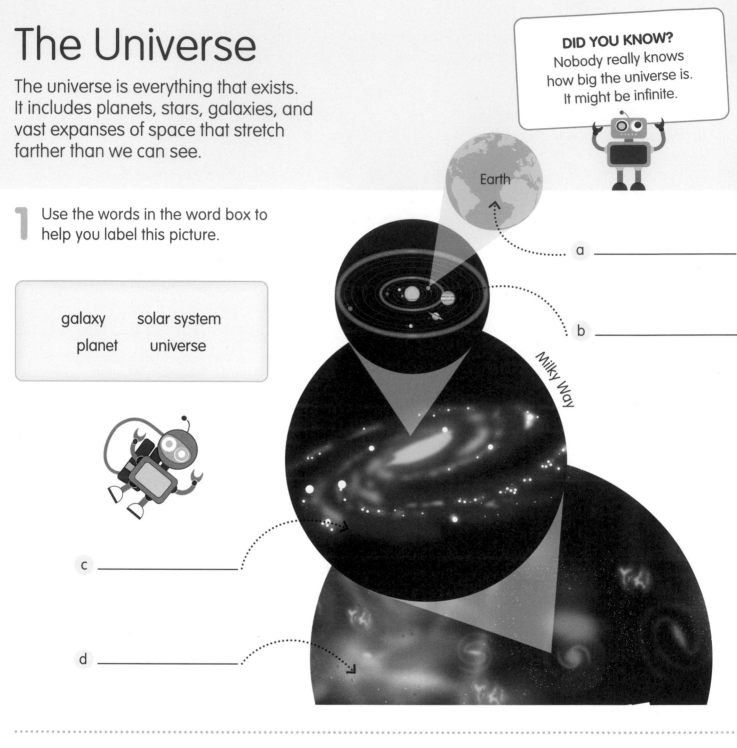

Earth

a _____

b _____

Milky Way

c _____

d _____

2 List the words from the word box in question 1 in order of size, from the largest to the smallest.

a _____   b _____   c _____   d _____

Largest ⟶ Smallest

3 Answer these questions about our galaxy and solar system.

a What is the name of our galaxy? _____

b How many stars are there in our galaxy: 100, a million, billions? _____

c What is the name of the star at the center of our solar system? _____

d What is the name of our planet? _____

e What is the name of the outermost planet in our solar system? _____

f What is the name of our local star? _____

4 Read these sentences about the universe and then circle true (T) or false (F) for each.

a We can only see part of the universe.   T / F

b The Milky Way is 140,000 km wide.   T / F

c We use light years to measure distance because the universe is light.   T / F

d The sun is the only star in the Milky Way.   T / F

e The planets in our solar system orbit the sun.   T / F

REMEMBER!
Distances in the universe are immense, so astronomers use light years to measure them. A light year is the distance that light travels in one year.

5 Circle the correct words to complete each of these sentences about measurements.

a One light year is **9.5 trillion km / 9.5 billion km / 9.5 million km**.

b The Milky Way is **1,400 / 140,000 / 1,400,000** light years wide.

c Traveling at the speed of light, it would take ½ / ¼ / ⅐ of a second to travel around Earth.

d Traveling at the speed of light, it would take **4.5 hours / 41 hours / 4 days** to reach Neptune from Earth.

e There are **400 / 400 million / 400 billion** stars in the Milky Way.

f Traveling at the speed of light, it would take **1 hour / 1 minute / 1 second** to reach the moon.

g There are around **10 million / 100 million / 100 billion** galaxies in the observable universe.

h The observable Universe is over **90 million km / 90 billion light years / 90 billion km** wide.

Pages 268–269

The solar system

Our solar system consists of a star—our sun—and the objects that orbit, or travel, around it. The solar system includes eight planets and their moons as well as asteroids, comets, and dwarf planets.

DID YOU KNOW?
The sun and the rest of our solar system formed about 4.5 billion years ago.

1 Use the words in the word box to help you label these objects in our solar system.

Saturn	Jupiter	Uranus	Neptune	Venus	sun	Earth
Mercury	Mars	comet	asteroid belt	Kuiper Belt		

l _____

a _____

c _____

j _____

d _____

h _____

i _____

e _____

g _____

k _____

b _____

f _____

2 Use the words in the word box to help you complete these
sentences about the different parts of our solar system.

asteroid belt   giant planets   comet   dwarf planet   sun   Kuiper Belt   rocky planets

a   The _____ are Mercury, Venus, Earth, and Mars, which are made of rock and metal.

b   The _____ is a ring of asteroids (made of rocks) orbiting the sun.

c   The _____ are Jupiter, Saturn, Uranus, and Neptune, which are made of gas.

d   A _____ is a lump of rock, ice, and dust that orbits the sun.

e   The _____ is a ring of comets on the outer reaches of the solar system.

f   The _____ is the star at the center of the solar system.

g   A _____ , such as Pluto, is an object in space that is like a very small planet.

3 Circle the correct words or phrases
to complete each of these sentences
about the solar system.

a   **Eight / Nine** planets orbit the sun.

b   **Neptune / Mars** is made mostly
of helium and hydrogen.

c   **Earth / Pluto** is a small
dwarf planet.

d   **Saturn / Venus** is made of rock
and is a solid planet.

e   **Mercury / Jupiter** is a very, very
big planet.

f   **The moon / Saturn** is a planet
with rings of ice and dust.

g   The **Kuiper Belt / asteroid belt**
orbits between Mars and Jupiter.

4 Read these statements about our solar system
and then circle true (T) or false (F) for each.

a   The planets in the solar system   T / F
orbit the sun.

b   Our solar system is just a star   T / F
and its planets.

c   The sun is the biggest object   T / F
in our solar system.

d   All the objects stay in their orbits   T / F
because of the moon's gravity.

e   Comets produce bright tails when   T / F
they get close to the sun.

f   The planets are spherical   T / F
because of gravity.

g   All the planets are made   T / F
partly of metal.

Pages 270–271

The sun

The sun is our local star, and it has been shining for about 4.6 billion years. It is a glowing ball of extremely hot gas—mostly hydrogen.

REMEMBER!
Never look directly at the sun either with your naked eye or through binoculars—it's dangerous!

1 Read these descriptions of the sun and check the ones that are true.

a The sun is a star. ☐

b The sun is a planet. ☐

c The sun is solid. ☐

d The sun is made of gas. ☐

e The sun has existed for about 4.6 million years. ☐

f The sun is hotter on the outside than in the middle. ☐

g The sun is at the center of the solar system. ☐

h The sun is on the edge of the solar system. ☐

2 Number these sentences to match the correct layers shown on the diagram of the Sun.

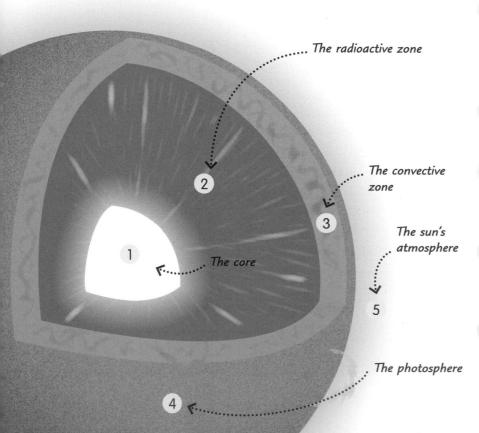

The radioactive zone — 2

The convective zone — 3

The sun's atmosphere — 5

The core — 1

The photosphere — 4

a The temperature in this layer reaches 16 million°C. Nuclear reactions release light and other forms of radiation. ☐

b Vast bubbles of hot gas rise to the surface, releasing energy. ☐

c Loops of hot gas called prominences erupt into the atmosphere. ☐

d Energy from the core slowly travels up through this layer. ☐

e Vast amounts of light, heat, and other radiation are emitted from here. ☐

3 This diagram shows what will happen to the Sun in the distant future. Use the diagram and the words in the word box to help you complete the sentences on the right.

hydrogen	white dwarf
planets	red giant	five billion

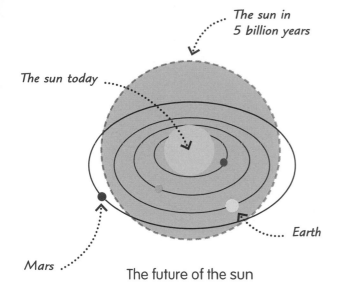

The sun in 5 billion years

The sun today

Mars

Earth

The future of the sun

a In _____ years, the sun will start to run out of _____ .

b Then, it will swell up and become a _____ .

c It will grow so big that it will swallow the nearest _____ .

d Then, it will disintegrate, leaving a _____ star.

4 Answer these questions about auroras.

a Where can you see auroras?

_____

b When can you see them?

_____

c What causes them?

_____

d What do they look like?

_____

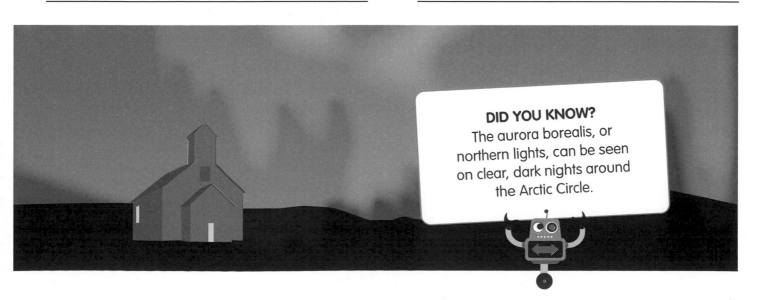

DID YOU KNOW?
The aurora borealis, or northern lights, can be seen on clear, dark nights around the Arctic Circle.

Pages 274–275

The planets

Our solar system's eight planets are divided into two types. The innermost four are rocky planets—balls of rock and metal. The outer four are giant planets, made of gas, liquid, and ice.

DID YOU KNOW?
The largest planet in our solar system is Jupiter (143,000 km across), and the smallest is Mercury (4,880 km across).

1 Draw lines to match each piece of information with the correct rocky planet. There are two pieces of information for each planet.

a   Mercury

c   Earth

A dusty, desert world

Covered in volcanoes

Extremely hot

Has life

Has lots of craters

Smallest planet

Has liquid water

b   Venus

d   Mars

2 Use the words in the word box to help you complete these sentences about the atmospheres of rocky planets. You will need to use some words twice.

carbon dioxide
hardly any   thick, yellow
thin   oxygen-rich

a   Mercury has _____ atmosphere.

b   Earth has an _____ atmosphere.

c   Venus has a _____ atmosphere made of _____ .

d   Mars has a _____ atmosphere made of _____ .

3 Use the words in the word box to help you label the four gas giants.

| Jupiter   Uranus   Neptune   Saturn |

a _____

Fastest-spinning planet

b _____

Surrounded by
frozen methane

c _____

Surrounded by
vast rings

d _____

Spins on its side

DID YOU KNOW?
Mercury, Venus, Mars, Jupiter,
and Saturn can all be seen from
Earth with the naked eye.

4 Check the correct definitions for each of these terms.

a The "Goldilocks" zone:

The area around a star where
it is neither too hot nor too cold
for life to exist. ☐

The area around a star where
most of the planets orbit. ☐

b Meteorite craters:

Craters on the surface of
a planet caused by meteorites
hitting it. ☐

Meteorites that are covered
in craters. ☐

c Dwarf planets:

Planets that are so small,
we can't see them. ☐

Small planets that have
only enough gravity to
keep themselves spherical. ☐

d Turbulent weather systems:

Areas of strong winds and
violent storms. ☐

Hot days and cold days. ☐

Gravity and orbits

Gravity is the force of attraction that pulls falling objects to Earth. Gravity keeps the moon in orbit around Earth and the planets in orbit around the sun.

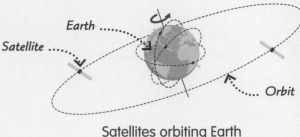

Satellites orbiting Earth

1 Draw lines to match these sentence halves about gravity.

a [All objects with mass]   [have enough gravity to pull things strongly.]

b [Only things with a huge mass]   [the stronger the pull of its gravity.]

c [The greater the mass of an object,]   [exert the force of gravity.]

d [If you throw something up in the air,]   [are kept in place by the sun's gravity.]

e [All the objects in the solar system]   [the gravity exerted by Earth pulls it down.]

SCIENCE AT HOME

Gravity and orbiting

You will need a bucket, a piece of stretchy fabric, a tennis ball, a marble, and some elastic or string.

1. Stretch the fabric over the top of the bucket and tie it with some elastic or string. This represents space.

2. Roll the marble onto the fabric. The marble represents Earth. How does it move—in a straight or curved line?

3. Remove the marble and drop the tennis ball into the middle of the fabric so that it sinks slightly. The tennis ball represents the sun.

4. Now, roll the marble onto the fabric. How does it move?

2 Answer these questions about orbits.

a What is an orbit? _____

_____

_____

b What causes orbits? _____

_____

c What shape is an orbit? _____

_____

d How is an object in orbit like a ball somebody

has thrown? _____

_____

3 Draw lines to match each picture with the correct description about the effects of gravity. Each picture has two descriptions.

An object follows a curved path as gravity pulls it back to Earth.	The sun's gravity keeps all the objects moving around it.	A huge amount of mass at the core creates gravity across a vast expanse of space.	Gravity pulls the gas inward, forming a sphere.

 a 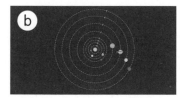 b  c 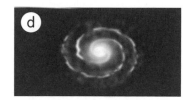 d

Gravity keeps the eight planets in orbit.	Gravity crushes gas atoms, creating heat and light.	A vast amount of mass at the center keeps billions of stars in orbit.	Gravity makes objects fall to the ground.

4 Underline the correct answers to these questions about orbits and gravity. Use the diagram to help you.

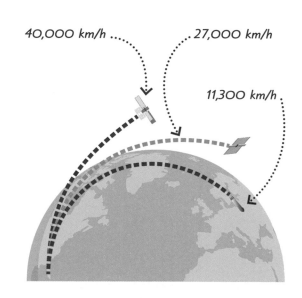

a   What happens to an object moving at less than 11,300 km/h?
It goes into outer space / It falls back to Earth

b   What happens to an object moving at 27,000 km/h?
It goes into outer space / It goes into orbit

c   What happens to an object moving faster than 40,000 km/h?
It goes into orbit / It goes into outer space

40,000 km/h   27,000 km/h

11,300 km/h

📖 Pages 276–277

Earth and the moon

The moon is a satellite of Earth. It orbits Earth once every 27.3 days. It doesn't produce its own light, but we can see it because it reflects light from the sun.

REMEMBER!
The moon appears to change shape as it orbits Earth. These different shapes are called phases.

1 Look at this diagram of the moon orbiting Earth and then use it to help you to color in the part of the moon that cannot be seen from Earth in each phase below.

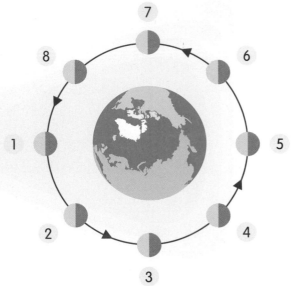

1   2   3   4   5   6   7   8

2 Read these sentences about the moon and then circle true (T) or false (F) for each.

a   The moon doesn't really change shape.   T / F

b   The moon produces light and heat.   T / F

c   The moon takes almost a month to orbit Earth.   T / F

d   A full moon is when the moon is on the opposite side of Earth from the sun.   T / F

e   A new moon is when we can see the whole moon.   T / F

f   The phases of the moon are caused by gravity.   T / F

3 Use the words in the word box to help you label this diagram of a solar eclipse. Then, use a darker and a lighter shade to color in the parts of the moon's shadow that will create a total eclipse and a partial eclipse on Earth.

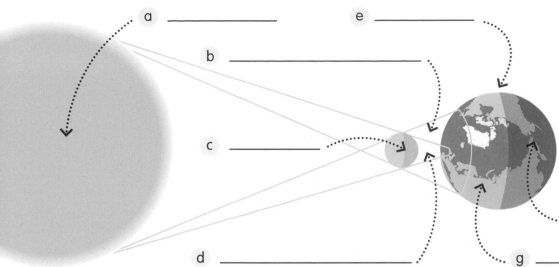

a _____

b _____

c _____

d _____

e _____

f _____

g _____

Moon

Earth

Sun

Partial solar eclipse

Total solar eclipse

Daytime

Nighttime

4 Answer these questions about eclipses.

a What is an eclipse?

_____

b What casts a shadow on the surface of Earth during a solar eclipse: the sun or the moon?

_____

c If you are in a total eclipse of the sun, what can you see?

_____

d What is the difference between a total solar eclipse and a partial solar eclipse?

_____

e Why shouldn't you look directly at the sun?

_____

SCIENCE AT HOME

Is the moon getting bigger or smaller?

1. Hold your hands up and make a crescent shape with each hand.

2. If the visible part of the moon fits into your left hand, the moon is getting smaller. If it fits into your right hand, the moon is getting bigger.

3. Look at the moon tonight. Is it getting smaller or bigger, or can you see the whole moon?

_____

📖 Pages 278–279

How fossils form

Fossils are the remains of animals, plants, and other living things, preserved in rocks. They range from microscopic traces of bacterial cells to gigantic dinosaur bones and tree trunks that have turned to rock.

DID YOU KNOW?
The oldest fossils that have been discovered are bacteria. They are 3.5 billion years old.

1 Number these pictures in the correct order to show how fossils form. Then, number the descriptions below to match the pictures. Each picture has two descriptions.

a ☐

b ☐

c ☐

d ☐

e　Only the skeleton is left. It is covered in a layer of sediment. ☐

f　An animal dies in a lake, and its body is buried in sand and mud. ☐

g　Over millions of years, more layers of sediment form. ☐

h　The soft parts of its body are consumed or decay. ☐

i　The layer with the fossils is raised upward when Earth's crust moves. ☐

j　The weight of the layers fuses the sediment together, and the skeleton is encased in rock. ☐

k　The top layer is eroded. ☐

l　The bones turn to rock. ☐

2 Use the words in the word box to help you complete this information about fossils and their formation.

crust	erode	fossils	layer
life	millions	raised	revealed

Only a very small number of animals and plants leave _____ behind. Fossils are

rare because they form over _____ of years. They tell us about the history of

_____ on Earth. Fossils are discovered when the _____ they are

buried in is _____ as Earth's _____ moves. Then, water and ice

_____ the layers of sediment until the fossils are _____ .

3 Use the words in the word box to help you label these different types of fossils.

carbon film

dung fossil

footprint fossil

fossil in amber

mold fossil

petrified shell

a _____

b _____

c _____

d _____

e _____

f _____

4 Answer these questions about the fossils in question 3.

a Which type of fossil belongs to a marine animal? _____

*b Which type of fossil belongs to an insect trapped in tree sap? _____

c Which type of fossil is waste produce from animals? _____

d Which type of fossil is a mark left by an animal? _____

e Which type of fossil is an impression of the original shape of an animal? _____

f Which type of fossil is a thin layer of carbon deposited on rock? _____

Pages 290–291

Rocks and minerals

Earth's crust is formed of many types of rock.
These rocks are made of crystallized chemicals
known as minerals. We use minerals to make
all sorts of things, from jewelry to buildings.

REMEMBER!
Minerals vary in their
hardness, from very soft
to very hard.

1 Read these sentences about rocks and then circle true (T)
or false (F) for each.

a   Rocks are collections of mineral crystals cemented together.   T / F

b   Rocks are only made of one type of crystal.   T / F

c   Chalk is a metamorphic rock.   T / F

d   Sedimentary rocks form at or near Earth's surface.   T / F

e   All rocks are igneous.   T / F

f   Igneous rocks are created by volcanoes.   T / F

2 Circle nine words about rocks, minerals, and fossils in the word
search below. Use the words in the word box to help you.

z	m	e	t	a	m	o	r	p	h	i	c	g	y
r	i	x	g	n	e	i	s	s	k	g	q	r	t
u	n	h	z	p	a	t	t	e	r	n	s	a	r
r	e	u	y	v	w	g	d	b	p	e	z	n	s
c	r	f	o	s	s	i	l	s	y	o	r	i	i
e	a	t	g	z	x	v	y	c	a	u	k	t	p
y	l	i	m	e	s	t	o	n	e	s	m	e	r
z	s	e	d	i	m	e	n	t	a	r	y	k	a

fossils

gneiss

granite

igneous

limestone

metamorphic

minerals

patterns

sedimentary

3 Use some of the words from the word box in question 2 to complete this information about rocks.

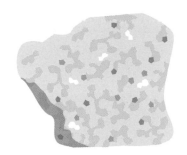

a Limestone is a

_____ rock.

It often contains

_____ .

b Pink granite is an

_____ rock.

It contains four different

types of _____ .

c Gneiss is a

_____ rock.

It has _____

caused by heat and pressure.

4 Draw lines to match these pictures of minerals with the correct descriptions.

a

b

c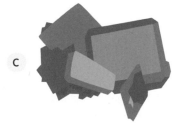

Aragonite has
needlelike crystals.

Hematite is silvery gray
and has a lumpy shape.

Gold is bright yellow
and quite soft.

Pyrite has shiny,
cube-shaped crystals.

Quartz has long,
hexagonal crystals.

Wulfenite has flat,
orange crystals.

d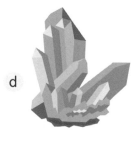

e

f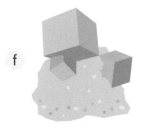

Pages 286–287

The water cycle

The amount of water on Earth never changes—it just gets recycled. Water is always moving between the sea, air, and land, going around and around in a never-ending cycle.

REMEMBER!
Precipitation is when water falls back to the ground.

1 Add arrows to this diagram of the water cycle to show how water moves around Earth.

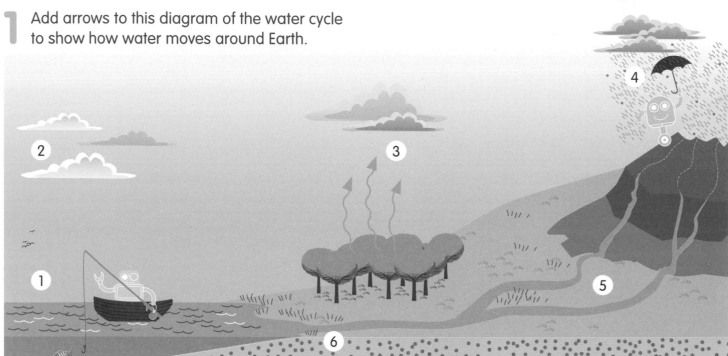

2 Read these sentences about the water cycle and then number them to match the correct stages in the diagram in question 1. You will need to use some numbers twice.

a   Water condenses into water droplets and forms clouds. ☐

b   Some water seeps underground and makes its way to the sea. ☐

c   The water vapor rises and cools. ☐

d   The water evaporates into the air. ☐

e   The water from rain and snow runs over the land. ☐

f   The water joins rivers and flows into the sea. ☐

g   The Sun heats water on Earth's surface. ☐

h   Trees and other plants release water vapor from their leaves. ☐

i   Water droplets join together to form bigger drops. ☐

j   When the drops get too heavy, they fall as rain. ☐

3 Use the words in the word box to help you complete this information about the water cycle.

liquid	condensation	evaporation
the sun	solid	transpiration	gas

a The three different states of water:

_____   _____   _____

b The two processes involved in changing states of water:

_____   _____

c The source of energy for the water cycle: _____

d The process by which plants release water vapor into the air: _____

4 Look at these pictures, then label the type of precipitation shown in each.

a _____   b _____

5 Answer these questions about how we get salt from seawater. Use the diagram on the right to help you.

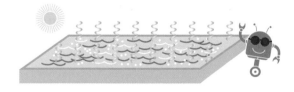

a Where do we store the water for extracting salt? _____

b Does the water evaporate or condense? _____

c What makes this happen? _____

d What is left behind? _____

📖 Pages 296–297

Rivers

Most of the rain or snow that falls on land finds its way into rivers. Over time, rivers transform Earth's landscapes, carving out valleys and depositing sediment in floodplains and deltas.

REMEMBER!
A river doesn't have a single source. It collects rain from a large area called a drainage basin or catchment area.

1 Use the words in the word box to help you label the features of this river system.

oxbow lake   salt marsh

glacier   waterfall   mountain lake

rapids   rain and snow

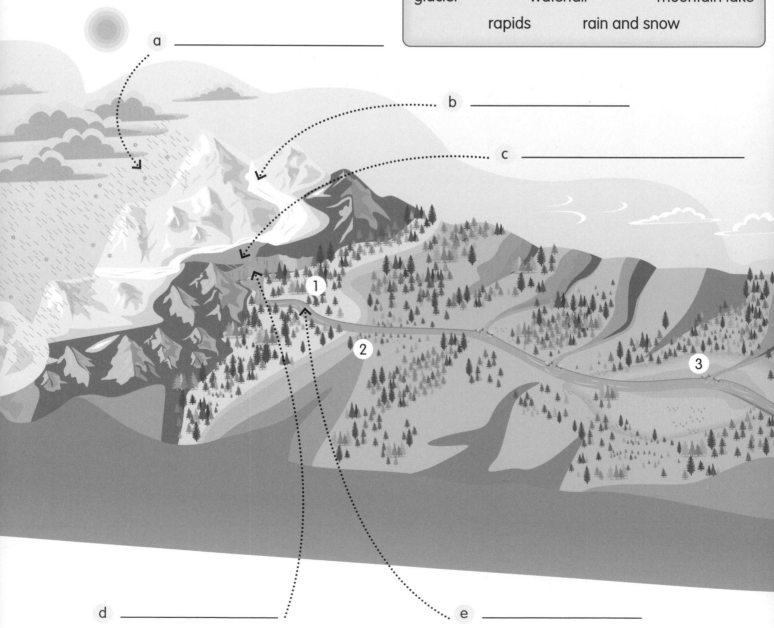

a _____

b _____

c _____

d _____   e _____

2 Read these sentences about the parts of a river and then number them to match the correct stages on the diagram below.

a The floodplain is a flat, low-lying area that surrounds a river and gets covered in water when the river overflows. ☐

b A meander is an S-shaped loop that forms as a river nears the sea. ☐

c Rapids are torrents of water formed from the meltwater from snow. ☐

d A tributary is a smaller river that flows into the main river. Tributaries add more and more water to the river as it flows toward the sea. ☐

e The mouth of the river is where it meets the sea and sediment is deposited. ☐

f A river valley is created by water eroding the land over millions of years. ☐

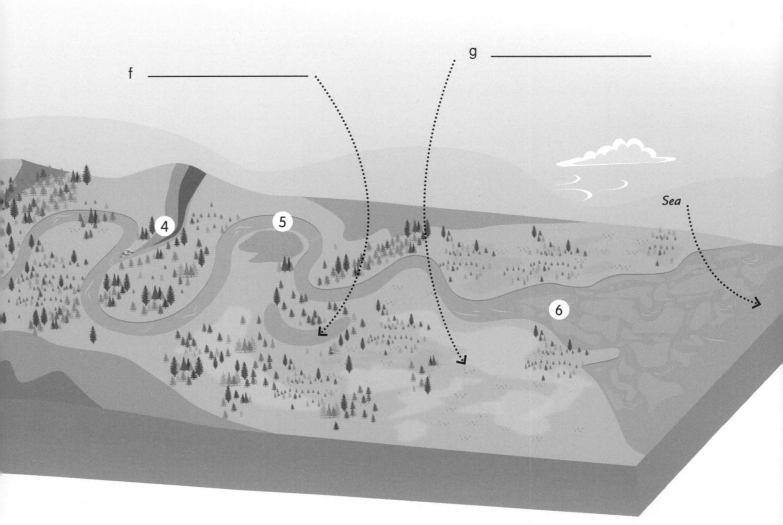

Glaciers

Glaciers are masses of ice found in mountain ranges and polar regions. As they flow slowly downhill, they wear away the ground below, gradually changing the landscape.

REMEMBER!
Over time, glaciers turn steep-sided river valleys into wide, U-shaped valleys.

1 Use the words in the word box to help you label the different parts of the glacier.

tributary glacier   accumulation zone   meltwater channel

ablation zone   rocks deposited by glacier   fallen rocks on surface   terminal moraine

bowl-shaped hollow   crevasses

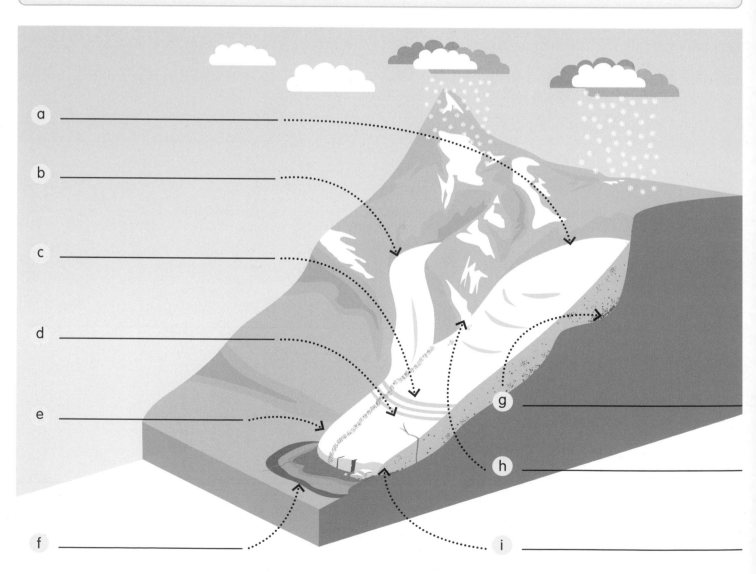

a _____

b _____

c _____

d _____

e _____

f _____

g _____

h _____

i _____

2 Number these sentences in the correct order to explain how a glacier
travels down a mountainside.

a   The glacier carries rocks that get dragged along, scraping the bottom of the valley. ☐

b   A crescent-shaped pile of rocks, called a moraine, is created at the foot of the glacier. ☐

c   The ice erodes a hollow shape in the mountain. ☐

d   Giant cracks (crevasses) and meltwater channels crisscross the surface of the glacier. ☐

e   The ice begins to melt in the ablation zone. ☐

f   Snow piles up in the accumulation zone at the top of the mountain. ☐

g   The body of the glacier flows slowly downhill. ☐

3 When a glacier melts and disappears, it leaves behind
marks on the landscape. Use the words in the word box
to help you complete the sentences below.

| erratic | kettle lake |
| esker | drumlin |

a   A _____ is a hill
made of loose rocks deposited
by the glacier.

b   A _____ is a shallow,
circular lake that is left when a lump
of ice melts.

c   An _____ is a
massive boulder all on its own,
which was dumped by a glacier.

d   An _____ is a winding
ridge of gravel left by a stream
running under a glacier.

Pages 300–301

Weather

The air and water in Earth's atmosphere are always on the move, driven by the sun's energy and Earth's rotation. These movements create wind, rain, and other types of weather.

REMEMBER!
A lot of the changing weather we experience is due to masses of air moving and colliding.

1 Look at these pictures, read the statements below, and then check the weather condition described in each one.

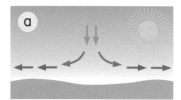

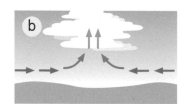

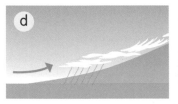

Air from high up in the atmosphere presses on the air below.

Air cools as it rises, and moisture in the air condenses to form clouds.

A mass of cold air pushes up warm air.

A mass of warm air slides over cold air.

| High pressure ☐ | High pressure ☐ | Cold front ☐ | Cold front ☐ |
| Low pressure ☐ | Low pressure ☐ | Warm front ☐ | Warm front ☐ |

2 Draw lines to match each picture of extreme weather conditions to the correct description.

Hurricanes are huge revolving storm systems that form over tropical oceans.

Electrical storms involve thunder, lightning, strong winds, and heavy rain.

Blizzards are severe storms with heavy snowfall and high winds.

Heatwaves involve unusually hot weather that destroys crops.

Climate zones

Climate is the typical pattern of weather that a place experiences over a period of time. We divide Earth into climate zones that represent the normal weather conditions for each zone.

Some parts of the world have rainy seasons and dry seasons instead of summer and winter.

1 Use the words "tropical," "polar," or "temperate" to label this diagram showing climate zones.

a _____ zone _____

b _____ zone _____

c _____ zone _____

d _____ zone _____

e _____ zone _____

f _____ zone _____

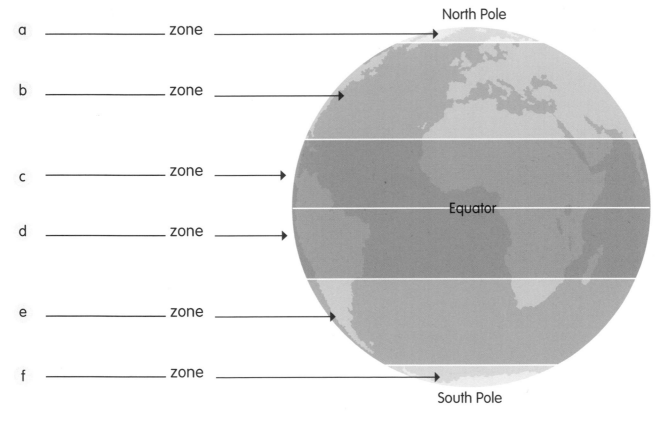

North Pole

Equator

South Pole

2 Read these statements about climate zones and then circle true (T) or false (F) for each.

a There are only two seasons in the polar zones.   T / F

b The climate in the tropical zones is hot and dry.   T / F

c Along the equator, it is rainy all year round.   T / F

d The polar zones are the hottest parts of Earth.   T / F

e In the temperate zones, the average temperatures are mild.   T / F

f Earth's shape and tilt create the climate zone.   T / F

📖 Page 303

Answers

6–7 How science works

1. (a) Step 1: make an observation
   (b) Step 2: form a hypothesis
   (c) Step 3: do an experiment
   (d) Step 4: collect data
   (e) Step 5: analyze results
   (f) Step 6: repeat the experiment

2. (a) Step 4   (b) Step 2   (c) Step 1
   (d) Step 3   (e) Step 5   (f) Step 6

3. (a) Observation: look and notice something.
   (b) Hypothesis: an explanation for something.
   (c) Experiment: test to find something out.
   (d) Data: facts and figures.
   (e) Analyze: examine something carefully.
   (f) Repeat: do something again.

4. (a) A plant, a light place and a dark place, water, soil
   (b) The window ledge, the bookshelf
   (c) The window ledge, because the plant will get most light there.

8–9 Working scientifically

1. (a) S (b) C (c) C (d) S (e) C (f) S
   (g) C (h) S

2. (c)

3. (a) F (b) F (c) T (d) T (e) T (f) T

4. Check all

Science at home Learner's own answers.

10–11 Fields of science

1.

t	f	e	z	o	o	l	o	g	y	t	y	u	a
r	m	i	c	r	o	b	i	o	l	o	g	y	d
a	e	a	d	g	f	g	b	h	i	c	k	e	n
o	d	z	x	a	c	v	o	b	n	e	m	c	e
p	i	u	y	n	t	r	t	e	w	l	q	o	r
r	c	i	d	i	s	e	a	s	e	l	o	l	f
a	i	f	g	s	h	j	n	k	l	s	p	o	c
h	n	d	s	m	a	z	y	x	c	v	b	g	a
y	e	n	v	i	r	o	n	m	e	n	t	y	u

(a) zoology, botany   (b) ecology
(c) biology, cells   (d) medicine
(e) organism   (f) environment

2. (a) biology
   (b) physics
   (c) space science
   (d) Earth science
   (e) chemistry

3. (a) Biology: studies the relationship between animals and plants in an environment.
   (b) Chemistry: invents a new nonstick saucepan.
   (c) Earth science: identifies the rocks in a specific place.
   (d) Physics: calculates the force needed to move an object.
   (e) Space science: finds new planets and galaxies.

12–13 How engineering works

1. (a) civil   (b) electrical
   (c) mechanical   (d) chemical

2. (a) civil
   (b) electrical
   (c) mechanical
   (d) chemical
   (e) civil
   (f) chemical
   (g) electrical
   (h) mechanical

3.

4. (a) ask   (b) imagine   (c) plan
   (d) model   (e) test   (f) share

14–15 What is life?

1. (a) all   (b) some   (c) some   (d) some
   (e) all   (f) all   (g) some   (h) all

2. (a) get food   (b) reproduce   (c) grow
   (d) move   (e) get energy   (f) sense surroundings   (g) remove waste

3. (a) Move using muscles: H
   (b) Use energy: B
   (c) Urinate: H
   (d) Roots grow down: T
   (e) Give birth: H
   (f) Get bigger: B
   (g) Senses things in their surroundings: B
   (h) Create seeds: T

Science at home Learner's own answers.

16–17 Classification

1. (a) Animals: have sense organs, are multicellular, and eat other organisms.
   (b) Plants: are multicellular, produce their own food, and have roots.
   (c) Fungi: absorb food from organic matter.
   (d) Microorganisms: are microscopic, and some are single-celled.

2. (a) absorb
   (b) multicellular
   (c) single-celled
   (d) microscopic
   (e) organic matter

3. (a) T (b) F (c) T (d) F (e) T (f) F

4. Mammals: (a) (g) (j) (k)
   Birds: (a) (f) (j)
   Fish: (b) (d) (h) (i)
   Reptiles: (b) (c) (j)
   Amphibians: (b) (e) (h) (i)

18–19 Nutrition

1. (a) proteins
   (b) lipids
   (c) minerals
   (d) vitamins
   (e) carbohydrates
   (f) fiber

2. (a) Proteins: help repair tissues in the body.
   (b) Minerals: are important for teeth and bones.
   (c) Carbohydrates: provide energy for our cells.
   (d) Lipids: help our body store energy.
   (e) Fiber: keeps our digestive system healthy.
   (f) Vitamins: provide small amounts of compounds we need to stay healthy.

3. ⓐ Protein: some
Minerals: none
Carbohydrates: a lot
Vitamins: not a lot
Lipids: a lot
Fiber: none
ⓑ Protein: a lot
Minerals: a lot
Carbohydrates: some
Vitamins: a lot
Lipids: some
Fiber: a lot
ⓒ Protein: a lot
Minerals: some
Carbohydrates: a lot
Vitamins: some
Lipids: not a lot
Fiber: some

20–21 Human digestive system

1. ⓐ mouth
ⓑ liver
ⓒ gall bladder
ⓓ large intestine
ⓔ esophagus
ⓕ stomach
ⓖ pancreas
ⓗ small intestine

2.

r	o	s	s	w	t	s	i	s	x	v
c	s	e	c	r	e	t	e	d	v	q
i	r	s	a	b	s	o	r	b	e	d
y	r	y	s	f	a	e	c	e	s	w
p	e	r	i	s	t	a	l	s	i	s
n	s	a	l	i	v	a	y	u	n	s
a	d	e	n	z	y	m	e	s	p	i

3. ⓐ secreted, 4
ⓑ enzymes, 3
ⓒ saliva, 1
ⓓ feces, 6
ⓔ absorbed, 5
ⓕ peristalsis, 2

4. ⓐ In the mouth, food is mashed into small pieces.
ⓑ In the esophagus, food is pushed down a tube by muscles contracting and relaxing.
ⓒ In the stomach, food is churned up and mixed with acid.
ⓓ In the small intestine, food is mixed with enzymes that digest proteins, fats, and carbohydrates.

ⓔ In the large intestine, food is eliminated as waste and water is absorbed.

5. ⓐ First... a description of food being mashed in the mouth.
ⓑ Next... a description of food passing down the esophagus.
ⓒ Then... a description of food being mixed with the acid in the stomach.
ⓓ After that... a description of food passing through the small intestine and mixing with enzymes.
ⓔ Finally... a description of water being absorbed and waste expelled.

22–23 Teeth

1. ⓐ Incisors
ⓑ Molars
ⓒ Canines
ⓓ Premolars

2. ⓐ Carnivores eat other animals.
ⓑ Carnivores have molars to crunch through bones.
ⓒ Carnivores need canines to kill their prey and eat the meat.
ⓓ Herbivores eat a range of plants.
ⓔ Herbivores have molars for grinding tough vegetation.
ⓕ Herbivores need incisors for cutting through vegetation.

3. ⓐ T ⓑ F ⓒ T ⓓ T ⓔ F ⓕ T

4.

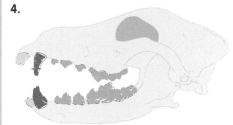
Dog skull

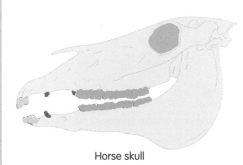
Horse skull

Science at home Learner's own answers.

24–25 Blood

1.

2.

a	b	b	l	o	o	d	v	e	s	s	e	l	s	f	e	i
q	h	r	d	o	x	e	e	a	r	t	e	r	i	e	s	f
c	e	a	s	d	y	k	i	y	r	p	g	d	s	u	h	l
a	a	c	t	n	g	b	n	c	h	a	m	b	e	r	s	y
m	r	z	a	j	e	r	s	v	u	a	s	e	w	b	h	x
p	t	m	v	c	u	c	a	p	i	l	l	a	r	i	e	s

3. ⓐ The heart is divided into left and right chambers.
ⓑ Arteries and veins are different types of blood vessels.
ⓒ Arteries travel out from the heart. Veins travel back to the heart.
ⓓ Arteries split into capillaries inside the tissues.

4. ⓐ Red blood cells
ⓑ White blood cells
ⓒ Platelets
ⓓ Plasma

5. ⓐ ✓ ⓒ ✓ ⓓ ✓ ⓕ ✓

26–27 The heart

1.

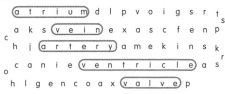

2. ⓐ vein
ⓑ right atrium
ⓒ valve
ⓓ right ventricle
ⓔ artery
ⓕ left atrium
ⓖ valve
ⓗ left ventricle

3. (a) When the heart relaxes, blood from the veins fills the atria. (b) The atrium walls contract and squeeze blood into the ventricles. (c) The ventricle walls contract, and blood moves out of the heart to the arteries.

4. (a) Four: left atrium, right atrium, left ventricle, right ventricle
(b) It flows into the atria and ventricles
(c) It flows out of the atria and ventricles
(d) The valves
(e) To the heart
(f) Away from the heart

28–29 Sensing and responding

1. (a) Because plants don't have a nervous system and muscles.
(b) Because foxes are predators and a danger to rabbits.

2. (a) stimulus
(b) control center
(c) receptors
(d) effectors
(e) response

3. (a) can
(b) don't have
(c) slowly
(d) toward
(e) touch
(f) always

4. (a) Rotten food: eyes, nose, mouth
(b) Fire: eyes, ears, nose, skin
(c) An approaching vehicle: eyes, ears
(d) Freezing ice cubes: eyes, skin

30 The human eye

1. (a) lens
(b) iris
(c) pupil
(d) cornea
(e) retina
(f) optic nerve

2. (a) 5
(b) 3
(c) 1
(d) 2
(e) 6
(f) 7
(g) 4

31 The human ear

1. (a) ossicles
(b) cochlear
(c) nerve
(d) eardrum

2. (a) cochlear
(b) eardrum
(c) nerve
(d) ossicles

32–33 How animals move

1. (a) Yes
(b) When muscles contract, they pull on parts of the body and make them move.
(c) Because they have muscles and a nervous system.
(d) From respiration

2. (a) fish, sides
(b) birds, wings
(c) insects, wings, legs
(d) mammals, legs

3. (a) Fish, Anemone, Earthworm
(b) Cheetah, Spider, Bird
(c) Bird, Bat, Bee
(d) Earthworm, Anemone

4. (a) Cheetahs move very quickly and are the fastest runners of all animals.
(b) Earthworms create a burrow as they move because they push through the soil.
(c) Sea anemones feed by catching prey in their tentacles.
(d) The muscles in the sides of a fish contract, causing the body to bend from side to side.

34–35 Muscles

1. (a) (b) (c) (g) (h)

2.

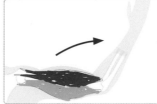

3. (a) skeletal muscle
(b) smooth muscle
(c) cardiac muscle

4. (a) IV
(b) IV
(c) V

5. (a) Skeletal muscles have long, slender fibers.
(b) Smooth muscles are found in the digestive system.
(c) Cardiac muscles keep working nonstop.
(d) Involuntary muscles work automatically.
(e) Voluntary muscles are controlled consciously.

36–37 Skeleton

1. (a) skull
(b) rib bones
(c) backbone
(d) hip bones
(e) hand bones
(f) limb bones
(g) foot bones

2. (a) hip bones
(b) skull
(c) rib bones
(d) backbone
(e) hand bones
(f) rib bones
(g) limb bones
(h) foot bones

3.

a strong
b hard
c light
d hollow
e long, straight
f curved

Science at home Learner's own answers.

38–39 Staying healthy

1. a yellow
b yellow
c red
d green
e red
f green

2. a c, e   b d, f   c a, b

3. a ✓   d ✓   e ✓

4. a Weight training
b Jogging
c Sprinting
d Gymnastics
e Cycling
f Ball games

Science at home Learner's own answers.

40–41 Animal reproduction

1. a male
b eggs
c one
d after
e inside
f different

2. a 6   b 1   c 4   d 8   e 7
f 3   g 5   h 2

3. a Sexual reproduction is: when there are two parents; when the offspring are all unique.

b Asexual reproduction is: when there is just one parent; when the offspring are genetically identical to the parents.

4. a Dividing—means splitting in two, forming identical animals with the same genes.
b Fragmentation—means dividing into fragments, which grow into whole new bodies.
c Asexual birth—means giving birth to clones, which are already pregnant with the next generation.

42 Life cycle of mammals

1. a 4: When they are adults
b 3: By playing and being curious
c 2: Their mother's milk
d 1: Inside their mother's uterus

2. a fetus
b litter
c adulthood
d milk
e partners
f uterus

43 Life cycle of birds

1. a adult birds
b eggs
c chicks
d caring for young

2. a male and female
b female
c male and female
d male and female

44–45 How eggs work

1. a shell
b air sac
c chalazae
d yolk
e embryo
f white

2. a shell
b air sac
c chalazae
d yolk
e embryo
f white

3. a limbs
b wings
c feathers
d tooth
e breath
f shell

4. a 9 days
b wings and a beak
c after 12 days
d after 21 days

46 Life cycle of amphibians

1. a eggs
b tadpoles
c develops legs
d froglet
e small frog
f adult frog

2. a froglet, adult frog
b tadpole
c froglet, adult frog
d tadpole
e froglet, adult frog
f froglet, adult frog
g tadpole, froglet
h tadpole, froglet, adult frog
i froglet, adult frog

47 Life cycle of insects

1. a Stage 2
b Stage 1
c Stage 6
d Stage 5
e Stage 4
f Stage 3
g Stage 6

2. a don't change
b have
c skin
d pupa

48–49 Growth and development

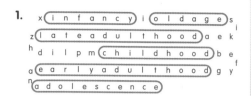

1.
- a infancy
- b childhood
- c adolescence
- d early adulthood
- e late adulthood
- f old age

2.
- a childhood
- b infancy
- c adolescence
- d old age
- e late adulthood
- f early adulthood

3.
- a From 10 to 12 years old.
- b Kashvi
- c 18
- d No, she didn't.

Science at home Learner's own answers.

50–51 Evolution

1.
- a Living organisms pass on genes to the next generation.
- b Offspring sometimes have variations in their genes.
- c The variations in genes affect the offspring's chances of survival.
- d The successful offspring pass on the variations to the next generation.

2.
- a Green beetle
- b Golden beetle
- c Pink beetle

3.
- a Archaeopteryx: teeth, front claws, back claws, feathers, bony tail, wings
- b Modern bird: back claws, feathers, tail with no bones, wings

4.
- a mutate
- b adapt
- c natural selection
- d variation
- e evolution
- f survival of the fittest

52–53 Plants

1. a T b F c T d F e F f T

2. a Roots b Leaf c Flower d Stem

3. a ✓ b ✓ d ✓ f ✓ g ✓
   h sunlight, water, soil, air, the right temperature

4.
- a the roots
- b the soil
- c the leaves
- d to make their food
- e the stem
- f to survive and stay strong
- g the flower
- h to reproduce

54–55 Types of plant

1.
- a seedling
- b flower
- c new seeds

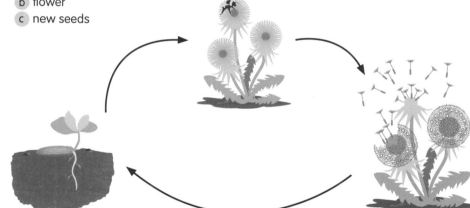

2. a a b a c c d b e b f c

3. a Mosses are small plants that grow in damp places. b Algae live in water. c Ferns have delicate leaves and live in shady places. d Conifers can be huge trees.

4.
- a mosses and algae
- b algae
- c mosses and algae
- d conifers, mosses, algae, and ferns
- e conifers
- f ferns, mosses, and algae
- g algae
- h mosses and algae

Science at home Learner's own answers.

56–57 Flowers

1.
- a pollen
- b stigma
- c stamen
- d carpel
- e ovary

2. c ✓ d ✓ e ✓

3.
- a 2
- b 4
- c 1
- d 3

4.
- a ovary
- b stamen
- c seeds
- d stigma
- e sex cells
- f fruit
- g seeds

58–59 Seed dispersal

1. a animal
b wind
c animal
d wind
e wind
f animal
g wind
h water

2. a bird
b squirrel
c rabbit

3. a sycamore
b pea
c dandelion
d poppy

4. a smaller
b can't
c further
d more
e some
f smaller

60–61 How seeds grow

1. A seed has a tough <u>outer coat</u> as protection. Inside the seed, there is a tiny baby plant called an <u>embryo</u>, which has a <u>root</u>, a <u>shoot</u>, and the <u>first true leaves</u>. There are also seed leaves inside the seed that are a <u>food store</u> for the plant.

2. a 4
b 3
c 2
d 4
e 1
f 3
g 2
h 1

3. a Place 1 is bad for germination because there isn't any water.
b Place 4 is bad for germination because there isn't much light.
c Place 6 is bad for germination because there isn't any soil.

Science at home Learner's own answers.

62–63 Asexual reproduction in plants

1.

```
w r u n n e r  r y u m s u c k e r q x i
r  r h i z o m e x z t u b e r q w a o z
s m c o r m w s d f p k j b z b u l b m z
s t o d t y q m i s p o p l a n t l e t k
t r w a s e x u a l s e e d s x z
```

a corm
b runner
c rhizome
d tuber
e plantlet
f sucker
g bulb
h asexual seeds

2. a rhizome
b tuber
c corm
d asexual seeds
e runner
f sucker
g bulb
h plantlet

3. 1 grafting 2 cutting

grafting: a 2 b 3 c 1

cutting: d 3 e 1 f 2

64–65 Single-celled organisms

1. a flagellum
b capsule (coat), pili
c DNA, cytoplasm
d cell, cell

2. a diatom
b Chlamydomonas
c chlorella

3. a 2, 6 b 4, 3 c 1, 5

4. a ~~Clean~~ Dirty
b ~~Moss~~ Bacteria
c ~~Soil~~ Water
d ~~Fish~~ Germs
e ~~Salty~~ Fresh

66–67 Food chains and recycling

1. 1 energy source
2 producers
3 primary consumers
4 secondary consumers
5 tertiary consumers
6 decomposers

2. a 3
b 5
c 6
d 2
e 1
f 4

3. a F
b T
c F
d F
e T
f F

4. a Mackerel: 2
b Shark: 1
c Algae: 4
d Shellfish: 3

5. a most
b decreases
c smaller
d more

68–69 Humans and the environment

1. a pollution—Some chemicals build up to toxic levels in the food chain.
b overexploitation—Animals are caught faster than they can reproduce.
c invasive species—New species replace native species.
d habitat loss—Habitats are cleared to make room for human needs.

2. a 2, 3, 4, 1
Type of threat: invasive species

b 3, 1, 4, 2
Type of threat: overexploitation

3. a b c d f

4. a Wheat, rice, maize b Many medicines originally come from plants.
c So they are resistant to disease and we have enough food.

70–71 States of matter

1. a solid b liquid c gas

2. a solid b liquid c solid d gas

3.

4. a Solid: toothbrush, fork
b Liquid: milk, honey
c Gas: oxygen, smoke

5. a Solids: have a fixed shape
b Liquids: can be poured and have no fixed shape c Gases: have no fixed shape and fill the whole container

72–73 Changing state

1. a melting
b evaporation
c freezing
d condensation
e solid
f liquid
g gas

2. a freezing
b melting
c evaporation
d condensation

3. a Freezing = liquid → solid
b Melting = solid → liquid
c Evaporation = liquid → gas
d Condensation = gas → liquid

4. a F b T c T d F e T

74–75 Properties of matter

1. a elastic
b strong
c malleable
d ductile
e flexible
f brittle
g hard

2. a hard
b brittle
c elastic
d malleable
e ductile
f flexible

3. a Hard materials are difficult to scratch.
b The hardness of a substance is measured using the Mohs scale.
c The Mohs scale compares materials to the hardness of 10 minerals.
d Minerals are rated on a scale of 1 to 10.
e Diamond is rated as 10, and talc is rated as 1.

4. a clay
b aluminum
c glass
d leather

76–77 Expanding gases

1. a 1 b 4 c 3 d 2

2. a less dense
b denser
c rises
d warmer
e cool
f closer together

3. a the sun
b the warm air on the ground transfers heat to it
c it rises
d because it is less dense
e it falls
f to help them fly

Science at home
1 air
2 the air warms up and rises, so the balloon inflates
3 the air cools down and falls so the balloon deflates
4 hot air rises and cold air falls

78–79 Mixtures

1. 1 solution
2 colloid
3 suspension

a 1 b 1 c 2 d 3 e 3 f 2

2. a gel
b emulsion
c aerosol
d foam
e jelly or similar
f mayonnaise or similar
g air freshener or similar
h whipped cream or similar

3. a Distilled water = pure chemical
b Iron sulfide = compound
c Iron filings and sulfur = mixture
d Brass = alloy
e Salt and pepper = mixture
f Bronze = alloy

4. a stir them together
b no
c no
d yes
e a mixture
f they are heated together to form a compound
g yes
h yes
i no
j a compound

80–81 Solutions

1. a solute
b solvent
c solid, spread out
d invisible
e some
f bottom

2. a saturated
b dilute
c because the molecules in the hot solvent mix more quickly
d to make the sugar dissolve more quickly

3. Circle: b Salt water c Fresh orange juice d Black coffee f Vegetable soup h Fizzy lemonade

4. a 3 b 1 c 2 d 4

Science at home Learner's own answers.

82–83 Separating mixtures 1

1. (a) Method: filtering. I can separate this mixture by pouring the mixture into the filter and letting the gravy drip through into another beaker.
(b) Method: decanting. I can separate this mixture by letting the oil rise to the top and the water sink to the bottom and then pouring off the water.
(c) Method: sieving. I can separate this mixture by shaking the mixture until the sugar falls through the sieve, leaving the nuts behind.

2. (a) sieve, sieve, sieving
(b) beaker, decanting
(c) filter, filter, filtering

3. (a) T (b) T (c) T (d) F (e) F

Science at home Learner's own answers.

84–85 Separating mixtures 2

1. (a) copper sulfate, water
(b) water
(c) gas
(d) evaporates
(e) solid

2. (a) In evaporation, we heat the solution to separate the chemicals.
In evaporation, the water escapes as gas.
In evaporation, only the solid residue is left.
(b) In distillation, we heat the solution to separate the chemicals.
In distillation, we heat and cool the solution to separate the chemicals.
In distillation, the resulting liquid is pure.

3. (a) Method: evaporation
Equipment: beaker, Bunsen burner
Stages: 1. Pour the salt water into the beaker and heat. 2. Continue boiling the salt water until all the liquid has evaporated and only salt remains in the beaker.

(b) Method: distillation.
Equipment: bottle, condenser, beaker, Bunsen burner.
Stages: 1. Pour the salt water into the bottle and heat. 2. Continue boiling the salt water until all the liquid has evaporated and passed through the condenser. 3. Collect the water in the beaker.

4. (a) gas
(b) liquid
(c) liquid
(d) solid
(e) liquid

86–87 Metals

1. cold, shiny, solid, hard, malleable, reflective, silvery

2. (a) most
(b) most
(c) all
(d) all
(e) most
(f) all

3. (a) gold
(b) copper
(c) mercury

4. (a) We use metal for cooking equipment because it is a good conductor of heat.
(b) We use metal for musical instruments because it makes a sound when it is struck.
(c) We use metal for electrical devices because it is a good electrical conductor.
(d) We use metal for making bridges because it is very strong. (e) We can make metal into thin sheets because it is malleable.

5. (a) mercury
(b) gold, silver
(c) aluminum
(d) copper
(e) lead
(f) iron

Science at home Learner's own answers.

88 Iron

1. (a) 3 (b) 1 (c) 4 (d) 2

2. (a) 1,000 BCE
(b) red
(c) tools
(d) carbon

89 Aluminum

1. (a) nontoxic
(b) thermal insulator
(c) malleable
(d) lightweight
(e) corrosion-proof

2. (a) 3
(b) 1
(c) 4
(d) 2
(e) 5

90 Silver

1. (b) ✓ (d) ✓ (f) ✓ (h) ✓

2. Antiseptic: kills bacteria
X-rays: light sensitive
Circuit board: good conductor
Jewelry: soft

3. (a) 2
(b) 1
(c) 4
(d) 3

91 Gold

1. (a) Because gold is found in rocks and needs to be washed out using acid or water.
(b) Because it doesn't react with oxygen at room temperature, so it doesn't tarnish.
(c) Because it is nontoxic.
(d) Because it doesn't react with oxygen in the air, so it doesn't corrode inside the components.
(e) Because it can be rolled into thin sheets and used to cover frames.

2. (a) T
(b) F
(c) T
(d) F
(e) F
(f) T
(g) F
(h) T

92–93 Carbon

1. (a) amorphous carbon
   (b) graphite
   (c) diamond
   (e) buckminsterfullerene

2. (a) A　(b) D　(c) B　(d) B　(e) D
   (f) G　(g) G　(h) A

3. (a) Carbon compounds from plants are used to make natural fibers such as cotton.—T-shirts and socks
   (b) Diamonds are very hard and strong and are used as blades in saws that can cut through concrete and even solid rock.—Diamond blade saw
   (c) Hydrocarbons are used in everyday products. For example, propane is used as a fuel in gas barbecues.—Propane canister
   (d) Fine plastic threads are woven together to make synthetic fibers such as polyester and nylon.—Fleeces and sleeping bags
   (e) Carbon fiber is used to make different types of vehicle because it is very light and very strong.—Racing bike

Science at home Learner's own answers.

94–95 Materials science

1. (a) multiple
   (b) flexible
   (c) strong

2. (a) clay
   (b) soft and malleable
   (c) they baked it
   (d) it becomes hard and brittle
   (e) ancient
   (f) bricks, tiles, pottery
   (g) insulators and coatings for a car engine
   (h) when the engine is running, it becomes very hot, so the parts need to be heat-resistant

3. (a) Windshields are made with two layers of glass and a layer of plastic in between: 1.
   (b) Tires are made with polyester and rubber and layered with steel cords: 3.
   (c) The bodies of some cars are made of threads of carbon woven and set into plastic to make carbon fiber: 2.

4. (a) Catalytic converters absorb toxic fumes from the exhaust: 5.
   (b) EDPM is a synthetic rubber used for waterproof trim around windows: 8.
   (c) Ceramic coatings can help piston heads withstand heat: 4.
   (d) Car seats are made of polyurethane, so they are light and stiff: 7.
   (e) Ceramic pressure sensors in tires tell the driver when to put more air in: 6.
   (f) Bumpers are made of a plastic called polypropylene, which is strong and easy to mold: 9.

96–97 Polymers

1. (a) cellulose
   (b) polythene
   (c) PVC
   (d) starch
   (e) casein
   (f) amino acids

2. (a) we break down the polymers into monomers　(b) sugar molecules joined together　(c) two polymers forming a double helix　(d) sugar molecules
   (e) thermoplastics, thermoset plastics
   (f) thermoplastics melt, thermoset plastics don't melt.

3. (a) Polythene　(b) PVC　(c) Polystyrene
   (d) Polycarbonate

4. (a) Polycarbonate plastic
   (b) Polystyrene
   (c) PVC
   (d) Polythene
   (e) Polycarbonate plastic
   (f) Polythene
   (g) PVC
   (h) Polystyrene

98–99 What is energy?

1. (a) heat, light: 1
   (b) chemical: 3
   (c) chemical: 2
   (d) kinetic: 6
   (e) kinetic, potential: 4
   (f) potential, kinetic: 5

2. (a) Chemical: battery
   (b) Electrical: electric pylon
   (c) Kinetic: sprinter off the blocks

   (d) Light: light bulb
   (e) Potential: sprinter on the blocks
   (f) Sound: musical instrument

3. (a) heat, light, sound
   (b) chemical, potential
   (c) light, chemical
   (d) sound, light, chemical

Science at home Learner's own answers.

100–101 Renewable energy

1. (a) wind
   (b) salt water
   (c) fresh water
   (d) plants
   (e) sunlight

2. (a) biomass　(b) solar power
   (c) wind power, hydroelectric power, tidal and wave power

3. (a) W　(b) T　(c) B　(d) S　(e) H

4. (a) biomass
   (b) hydroelectric
   (c) tidal and wave
   (d) wind
   (e) solar

5. (a) hydroelectric
   (b) by growing new crops and trees
   (c) solar
   (d) tidal and wave

102–103 Sound

1. (a) 2　(b) 4　(c) 1　(d) 5　(e) 3　(f) 6

2. (a) in all directions
   (b) they get farther apart
   (c) away from the source
   (d) the sound gets quieter
   (e) as vibrations
   (f) when the sound waves reach us

3. (a) as vibrations
   (b) vibrate the air molecules
   (c) liquid solid and gas
   (d) no
   (e) air molecules
   (f) a vacuum

4. (a) gas, 1
   (b) solid, 3
   (c) liquid, 2

104–105 Light

1. Emits light:
- (a) Sun
- (d) Candle
- (e) Light bulb
- (g) Fire
- (j) Torch

Reflects light:
- (b) Moon
- (c) Earth
- (f) Mirror
- (h) Disco ball
- (i) Window

2. (a) object
- (b) penumbra
- (c) light source
- (d) shadow
- (e) umbra

3. (a) opaque, no
- (b) translucent, some
- (c) transparent, almost all

Science at home Learner's own answers.

106–107 Reflection

1. (a)   (b)

SMOOTH SURFACE

ROUGH SURFACE

2. (a) Behind the mirror (b) The same distance as between me and the mirror

3. (a) T (b) T (c) F (d) F (e) T (f) F

4. (a) ✓ (c) ✓ (e) ✓ (f) ✓ (h) ✓

5. (a) CC (b) CV (c) CV (d) CV (e) CC
(f) CV (g) CV (h) CC (i) CC

108 Forming images

1. (a) virtual
- (b) real
- (c) magnifying
- (d) projector
- (e) pinhole
- (f) lens

2. (a) pinhole camera
- (b) camera
- (c) projector
- (d) C
- (e) PC
- (f) P
- (g) P
- (h) C
- (i) PC

109 Telescopes and microscopes

1. (a) eyepiece
- (b) focusing knob
- (c) object to be studied
- (d) lamp or mirror
- (e) object to be studied
- (f) eyepiece
- (g) objective lens
- (h) focusing dial

2. Microscope: (a) (d) (e)
Telescope: (b) (c) (f)

110–111 Colors

1. (a) 2 (b) 4 (c) 1 (d) 3

2. (a) green (b) all the other colors
(c) the leaf looks green

3. Circle the robot on the left, between sun and rainbow; (a) T (b) F (c) F (d) T (e) T

4. (a) red, blue, green
- (b) primary paint colors are red, blue, yellow
- (c) we get different colors
- (d) no
- (e) we get white

Science at home Learner's own answers.

112 Electromagnetic spectrum

1. (a) many different lengths
- (b) a small part of
- (c) radio waves
- (d) shorter
- (e) shorter
- (f) longer

2. (a) X-rays
- (b) ultraviolet
- (c) gamma rays
- (d) radio waves

113 Static electricity

1. Attract: (b) (d)
Repel: (a) (c)
Circle: (b) (d)

2. (b) (c) (e) (f)

114–115 Current electricity

1. Conductor:
- (a) Lemon juice
- (b) Tap water
- (c) Copper
- (f) Gold
- (g) Silver

Insulator:
- (d) Rubber
- (e) Cork
- (h) Wood
- (i) Wool
- (j) Paper

2. (a) T (b) F (c) F (d) T (e) F (f) T
(g) T (h) F

3. (a) copper
- (b) it's too expensive
- (c) because you will get an electric shock
- (d) because plastic picks up static electricity
- (e) plastic and rubber
- (f) water that has things dissolved in it

4. (a) cathode
- (b) positive charge
- (c) electrolyte
- (d) light bulb
- (e) anode
- (f) negative charge
- (g) battery

116–117 Electric circuits

1. Circle: battery, bulb, switch, wire

Color bulb in: (3) (5) (6)

2. (a) 6 (b) 4 (c) 5 (d) 1 (e) 3 (f) 2

3. (a) A completed circuit with a flowing electrical current. (b) There is more voltage for the bulb, so the light will be brighter. (c) There is less voltage for each bulb, so the light will be dimmer.
(d) The electrical current doesn't flow.

Science at home Learner's own answers.

118–119 What are forces?

1. a pushed
   b pulled
   c pushed
   d pulled
   e pushed

Science at home Learner's own answers.

2. a archer's arm, bend
   b bowstring, move
   c target, stop
   d leg, upward
   e gravity, fall

120–121 Stretching and deforming

1.
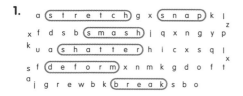

2. a elastic
   b plastic
   d brittle

3.
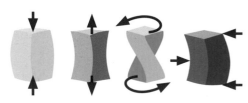

   a compression
   b tension
   c twisting
   d bending

4. a Stretching or deforming happens when forces act on an object that can't move.

b All objects break if enough force is applied to them.
c Brittle objects shatter or snap when forces act on them.
d Some objects change shape, and we say they deform.
e Forces act in different directions, and this produces different changes in shape.
f The way objects deform depends on the number and directions of the forces.
g Some forces called torques twist objects.
h Objects won't return to their original shape if you stretch them past their elastic limit.

122–123 Magnetism

1. a attract
   b north, south
   c push
   d pull
   e whole

2. a repel b repel c attract d Two magnets pull each other if opposite poles come close.

3. a A magnetic field
   b Curved
   c Two poles
   d Near the magnet
   e In the center of Earth
   f North

4. Circle: b c d
   g They are all made of metal.

Science at home Learner's own answers.

124–125 Friction

1. a slows things down
   b rub against
   c heat
   d wears away
   e slip on
   f increases

2. a walking in socks
   b skating on ice
   c pushing a box on a shiny surface

3. a it stops us from slipping everywhere
   b because objects that roll create less friction
   c the brakes

d some of the parts wear away
e add a lubricant
f the ones they use to wear away wood, such as a file

4. a The brakes exert friction on the wheels of the bike so that we can stop.
b There is friction between the surface of the road and the wheels. This stops us from slipping all over the road.
c There is friction between the pedals and our shoes so that our feet don't slip off the pedals.
d There is friction in the handlebars so that our hands can grip them.

126–127 Drag

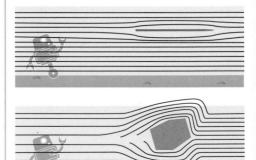

1.
a when moving objects push air molecules out of the way, they lose energy
b it slows them down
c because large objects have to move more molecules out of the way

2. a F b T c F d T e T f F

3. a sports car, airplane
   b dolphin, bird
   c bicycle, canoe

4. a 4 b 1 c 3 d 2

128–129 Simple machines

1. a Because we don't need to apply as much force, making the job easier.
b The amount by which the machine multiplies the force needed for a job.

2.

a

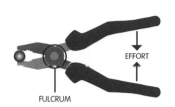

EFFORT

FULCRUM

b

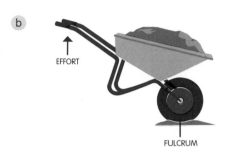

EFFORT

FULCRUM

c

FULCRUM

EFFORT

d

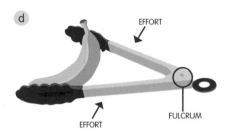

EFFORT

EFFORT

FULCRUM

EFFORT

3. (a) long, shallow, less
(b) short, steep, more

4. (a) $5 \div 2 = 2.5$
(b) $3 \div 2 = 1.5$

Science at home Learner's own answers.

130–131 **More simple machines**

1. (a) wheel and axle
(b) screw
(c) wedge
(d) pulley

2. (a) wedge
(b) screw
(c) wheel and axle
(d) pulley

3. (a) To move bags of soil in the garden.
(b) To place under a door to stop it from closing.
(c) To take the lid off a can of paint.

(d) To wheel a wheelchair into an entrance.
(e) To fix a shelf to the wall.
(f) To lift a pile of bricks to the roof of a house.

4. (a) lever, wedge
(b) wheel and axle, wedge
(c) lever, screw
(d) wheel and axle, lever

132–133 **Gravity**

1. (a) because the moon's gravity is less than Earth's (b) yes
(c) no (d) 0 N

2. (a) It is a force
(b) Everywhere in the universe
(c) Yes, it is

3. (a) mass
(b) weight
(c) accelerate
(d) pull
(e) more
(f) force

4. (a) T (b) T (c) F (d) F (e) T

134–135 **Flight**

1. (a) lift
(b) gravity
(c) it must accelerate very fast
(d) it rushes over wings
(e) it passes under the wings
(f) the front

2. (a) higher: 3
(b) more: 2
(c) higher: 1

3. (a) The short flaps on the wings are like brakes, and they increase the force of drag.
(b) The elevators are flaps at the back of the plane. They lift or drop the nose of the plane. (c) Ailerons are long flaps on the wings. They make the plane roll, which helps it turn. (d) The rudder is a flap on the tail. It makes the plane turn left or right.

Science at home Learner's own answers.

136–137 **Floating and sinking**

1. (a) 2 (b) 1 (c) 3 (d) 4

2. (a) sink, greater
(b) float, air, less
(c) air, water
(d) less

3. (a) 45 kg
(b) 17 kg
(c) 6 kg

4. (a) A submarine is surrounded by large spaces called ballast tanks.
(b) The ballast tanks can hold air or water.
(c) When the ballast tanks are full of air, the submarine floats.
(d) When the ballast tanks are full of water, the submarine sinks.
(e) Vents at the top control the air.
(f) The submarine is denser than the water when the ballast tanks are full of water.

138–139 **The universe**

1. (a) planet
(b) solar system
(c) galaxy
(d) universe

2. (a) universe
(b) galaxy
(c) solar system
(d) planet

3. (a) The Milky Way
(b) billions
(c) the sun
(d) Earth
(e) Neptune
(f) the sun

4. (a) T
(b) F
(c) F
(d) F
(e) T

5. (a) 9.5 trillion km
(b) 140,000
(c) $\frac{1}{7}$
(d) 4.5 hours
(e) 400 billion
(f) 1 second
(g) 100 billion
(h) 90 billion light years

140–141 The solar system

1. (a) sun
   (b) Mercury
   (c) Venus
   (d) Earth
   (e) Mars
   (f) asteroid belt
   (g) Jupiter
   (h) Saturn
   (i) Uranus
   (j) Neptune
   (k) comet
   (l) Kuiper Belt

2. (a) rocky planets
   (b) asteroid belt
   (c) giant planets
   (d) comet
   (e) Kuiper Belt
   (f) sun
   (g) dwarf planet

3. (a) Eight
   (b) Neptune
   (c) Pluto
   (d) Venus
   (e) Jupiter
   (f) Saturn
   (g) asteroid belt

4. (a) T
   (b) F
   (c) T
   (d) F
   (e) T
   (f) T
   (g) F

142–143 The sun

1. (a) ✓ (d) ✓ (g) ✓

2. (a) 1
   (b) 3
   (c) 5
   (d) 2
   (e) 4

3. (a) five billion, hydrogen
   (b) red giant
   (c) planets
   (d) white dwarf

4. (a) near the poles
   (b) at night
   (c) charged particles from the sun
   (d) ghostly patterns in the sky

144–145 The planets

1. (a) Has lots of craters; Smallest planet
   (b) Covered in volcanoes; Extremely hot
   (c) Has life; Has liquid water
   (d) A dusty, desert world;
   Has lots of craters

2. (a) hardly any
   (b) oxygen-rich
   (c) thick, yellow; carbon dioxide
   (d) thin; carbon dioxide

3. (a) Jupiter
   (b) Neptune
   (c) Saturn
   (d) Uranus

4. (a) The area around a star where it is neither too hot nor too cold for life to exist.
   (b) Craters on the surface of a planet caused by meteorites hitting it.
   (c) Small planets that only just have enough gravity to keep themselves spherical.
   (d) Areas of strong winds and violent storms.

146–147 Gravity and orbits

1. (a) All objects with mass exert the force of gravity.
   (b) Only things with a huge mass have enough gravity to pull things strongly.
   (c) The greater mass of an object, the stronger the pull of its gravity.
   (d) If you throw something up in the air, the gravity exerted by Earth pulls it down.
   (e) All the objects in the solar system are kept in place by the sun's gravity.

Science at home Learner's own answers.

2. (a) The path an object in space follows as it travels around another object
   (b) Gravity
   (c) Curved
   (d) Gravity makes it fall back to Earth

3. (a) An object follows a curved path as gravity pulls it back to Earth. Gravity makes objects fall to the ground.
   (b) The sun's gravity keeps all the objects moving around it. Gravity keeps the eight planets in orbit.
   (c) Gravity pulls the gas inward, forming a sphere. Gravity crushes gas atoms, creating heat and light.
   (d) Huge amounts of mass at the core create gravity across a vast expanse of space. Vast amounts of mass at the center keep billions of stars in orbit.

4. (a) It falls back to Earth
   (b) It goes into orbit
   (c) It goes into outer space

148–149 Earth and the moon

1.

a   b   c   d   e   f   g   h

2. (a) T
   (b) F
   (c) T
   (d) T
   (e) F
   (f) F

3. (a) Sun
   (b) Partial solar eclipse
   (c) Moon
   (d) Total solar eclipse
   (e) Earth
   (f) Nighttime
   (g) Daytime

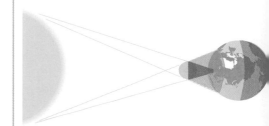

4. a When planets or moons cast shadows on each other
b The moon
c You can only see the outer circle of the sun
d In a total solar eclipse, you can't see the sun, and in a partial solar eclipse, you can only see part of the sun
e Because it can damage your eyes

Science at home Learner's own answers.

150–151 How fossils form

1. a 3
b 4
c 1
d 2
e 2
f 1
g 2
h 1
i 4
j 3
k 4
l 3

2. fossils, millions, life, layer, raised, crust, erode, revealed

3. a mold fossil
b petrified shell
c carbon film
d footprint fossil
e dung fossil
f fossil in amber

4. a petrified shell
b fossil in amber
c dung fossil
d footprint fossil
e mold fossil
f carbon film

152–153 Rocks and minerals

1. a T
b F
c F
d T
e F
f T

2.

```
z m e t a m o r p h i c g y
r i x g n e i s s k g q r t
u n h z p a t t e r n s a r
r e u y v w g d b p e z n s
c r f o s s i l s y o r i i
e a t g z x v y c a u k t p
y l i m e s t o n e s m e r
z s e d i m e n t a r y k a
```

3. a sedimentary, fossils
b igneous, minerals
c metamorphic, patterns

4. a Gold is bright yellow and quite soft.
b Aragonite has needlelike crystals.
c Wulfenite has flat, orange crystals.
d Quartz has long, hexagonal crystals.
e Hematite is silvery gray and has a lumpy shape.
f Pyrite has shiny, cube-shaped crystals.

154–155 The water cycle

1.

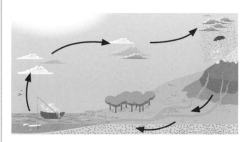

2. a 2 **b** 6 **c** 2 **d** 1 **e** 5 **f** 5 **g** 1 **h** 3 **i** 4 **j** 4

3. a solid, liquid, gas
b evaporation, condensation
c the sun
d transpiration

4. a snow
b rain

5. a in shallow pits
b it evaporates
c the heat from the sun
d salt

156–157 Rivers

1. a rain and snow
b glacier
c mountain lake
d waterfall
e rapids
f oxbow lake
g salt marsh

2. a 3 **b** 5 **c** 1 **d** 4 **e** 6 **f** 2

158–159 Glaciers

1. a accumulation zone
b tributary glacier
c crevasses
d meltwater channel
e ablation zone
f terminal moraine
g bowl-shaped hollow
h fallen rocks on surface
i rocks deposited by glacier.

2. a 4 **b** 7 **c** 2 **d** 5 **e** 6 **f** 1 **g** 3

3. a drumlin **b** kettle lake **c** erratic
d esker

160 The weather

1. a high pressure
b low pressure
c cold front
d warm front

2. a Hurricanes are huge revolving storm systems that form over tropical oceans.
b Heatwaves involve unusually hot weather that destroys crops.
c Electrical storms involve thunder, lightning, strong winds, and heavy rain.
d Blizzards are severe storms with heavy snowfall and high winds.

161 Climate zones

1. a polar **b** temperate
c tropical **d** tropical
e temperate **f** polar

2. a T **b** F **c** T **d** F **e** T **f** T